Federal Financial Institutions Examination Council

I0448855

ANNUAL REPORT 2008

Board of Governors of the Federal Reserve System, Federal Deposit Insurance Corporation, National Credit Union Administration, Office of the Comptroller of the Currency, Office of Thrift Supervision, State Liaison Committee

Members of the Council

Randall Kroszner, *Chairman*
Member, Board of Governors of the
Federal Reserve System

Sheila C. Bair, *Vice Chairman*
Chairman
Federal Deposit Insurance Corporation

John Munn
Director
Nebraska Department of Banking & Finance

John C. Dugan
Comptroller of the Currency
Office of the Comptroller of the Currency

Michael E. Fryzel
Chairman
National Credit Union Administration

John M. Reich
Director
Office of Thrift Supervision

LETTER OF TRANSMITTAL

Federal Financial Institutions
  Examination Council
Arlington, VA 22226
March 31, 2009

The President of the Senate
The Speaker of the House of Representatives

Pursuant to the provisions of section 1006(f) of the Financial Institutions Regulatory and Interest Rate Control Act of 1978 (12 U.S.C. § 3305), I am pleased to submit the 2008 Annual Report of the Federal Financial Institutions Examination Council.

Respectfully,

Daniel K. Tarullo

Daniel Tarullo
Chairman

TABLE OF CONTENTS

MESSAGE FROM THE CHAIRMAN

Randall Kroszner

I am pleased to report that the FFIEC continued its high level of performance and productivity throughout 2008. The Council continued to advance its mission of promoting uniformity and consistency in the supervision of financial institutions. The FFIEC also continued to foster communication, cooperation, and coordination among member agencies and the State Liaison Committee that make up the Council, and its task forces.

Details on the 2008 achievements are included later in this report in the Record of Council Activities (page 3) and Activities of the Interagency Staff Task Forces (page 7). I would like to cite here, however, some of the most significant initiatives by the Council, its task forces, and interagency working groups during the year:

- Adopted nine new and substantive changes to 14 existing interagency questions and answers on the Community Reinvestment Act in response to comments received to the revisions proposed in 2007. These questions and answers, published on January 6, 2009, consolidate and supersede all previously published interagency questions and answers.

- Revised examination procedures for Regulations M (Consumer Leasing) and Z (Truth in Lending) to comply with the E-Sign Act that each agency will incorporate into their examination programs.

- Approved Regulation DD (Truth in Savings) examination procedures to comply with regulatory changes on electronic disclosures and to incorporate the GAO's recommendation related to institutions providing disclosure information on bank fees to consumers.

- Updated interagency fair lending examination procedures, revising examination procedures and discrimination risk indicators for loan pricing, steering, and redlining, and including a discussion of mortgage brokers and associated fair lending risks.

- Approved the proposed updated compliance rating definitions that will be published for comment in the *Federal Register*, subject to agency approval.

- Established a Consumer Help Center on the FFIEC's website that assists consumers in identifying and reaching the appropriate regulator for consumer inquiries and complaints.

- Approved examination procedures to comply with regulatory changes on electronic disclosures as well as other amendments to Regulation E.

- Approved Fair Credit Reporting Act Examination procedures for Affiliate Marketing, Identity Theft Red Flags, and address discrepancies and reconciliation.

- Implemented a new process that allows UBPR Peer Group data to be published once all banks have filed their Call Report, which in turn allows UBPR reports to reflect peer group averages and percentile rankings sooner.

- Expanded loan yield information shown in the UBPR by taking advantage of new data in single family loans and other real estate loans, which should provide added insight into the contribution of real estate loans to bank profitability.

- Expanded information for restructured real estate loans and loans in foreclosure in the UBPR by taking advantage of new data in the Call Report, which should provide more information about bank loan quality.

- Established working groups to implement provisions of the SAFE Act (also known as Title V) which requires registration of mortgage lenders who work at financial institutions on the National Mortgage Licensing and Registration System.

- Continued work designed to help the agencies prepare for supervision in the event of a pandemic event. These projects included a Roundtable on Pandemic Planning and two emergency preparedness, response, and recovery meetings with industry representation.

- Updated the "Business Continuity Planning" booklet of the FFIEC's Information Technology Handbook series to include guidance on identifying the continuity planning that should be in place to minimize the potential adverse effects of a pandemic event.

- Sponsored an annual Information Technology conference for the agencies' examination staff to explore emerging risks and industry best practices.

- Conducted end-to-end Basel II data transfer tests between the Federal Reserve Board and other agencies. The next phase of testing will evaluate the data collection component.

- Trained over 2,600 state and federal employees from a variety of agencies through training sponsored by the FFIEC's Examiner Education Office, including continuation of the broad-based Supervisory Updates and Emerging Issues conferences and advanced instruction on credit analysis, cash flow construction, fraud, and anti-money laundering.

- Developed and produced a stand-alone, CD-based training product for agency personnel regarding the Financial Analysis of Technology Service Providers.

- Designed and piloted a timely and well-received course on Commercial Real Estate Analysis for Financial Institution Examiners.

- Continued work on long-term projects related to the Federal Reserve Board's new bulk data transfer facility, National Information Center (NIC) Architecture Redesign Initiative, and changes to NIC tables to implement the Structure Processing Application.

- Completed a secure, automated connection between the Federal Reserve Board and the National Credit Union Administration.

- Established a secure email link between the Office of Thrift Supervision and the Federal Reserve Board for supervisory documents.

I am extremely proud of the significant accomplishments that the FFIEC and its task forces achieved in 2008. I am pleased with our continued communication with other agencies as well. The communication channels and working relationships that the FFIEC fosters among agencies remains invaluable and is critically important during turbulent financial market conditions as we are currently experiencing. January 21, 2009 marks my last day with the Federal Reserve and it has been a pleasure and privilege to be able to chair the FFIEC during the last two years.

OVERVIEW OF THE FEDERAL FINANCIAL INSTITUTIONS EXAMINATION COUNCIL (FFIEC) OPERATIONS

The FFIEC was established on March 10, 1979, pursuant to title X of the Financial Institutions Regulatory and Interest Rate Control Act of 1978 (FIRIRCA), Public Law 95-630. The purpose of title X, entitled the Federal Financial Institutions Examination Council Act of 1978, was to create a formal interagency body empowered to prescribe uniform principles, standards, and report forms for the federal examination of financial institutions by the Board of Governors of the Federal Reserve System, the Federal Deposit Insurance Corporation, the National Credit Union Administration, the Office of the Comptroller of the Currency, and the Office of Thrift Supervision and to make recommendations to promote uniformity in the supervision of financial institutions. In accordance with the Financial Services Regulatory Relief Act of 2006, a representative state regulator was added as a member of the FFIEC in October 2006. The Council is also responsible for developing uniform reporting systems for federally supervised financial institutions, their holding companies, and the nonfinancial institution subsidiaries of those institutions and holding companies. It conducts schools for examiners employed by the five federal member agencies represented on the Council and makes those schools available to employees of state agencies that supervise financial institutions.

The Council was given additional statutory responsibilities by section 340 of the Housing and Community Development Act of 1980, Public Law 96-399. Among these responsibilities are the implementation of a system to facilitate public access to data that depository institutions must disclose under the Home Mortgage Disclosure Act of 1975 (HMDA) and the aggregation of annual HMDA data, by census tract, for each metropolitan statistical area.

Title XI of the Financial Institutions Reform, Recovery, and Enforcement Act of 1989 established the Appraisal Subcommittee within the Council. The functions of the subcommittee are (1) monitoring the requirements, including a code of professional responsibility, established by states for the certification and licensing of individuals who are qualified to perform appraisals in connection with federally related transactions; (2) monitoring the appraisal standards established by the federal financial institution regulatory agencies and the former Resolution Trust Corporation; (3) maintaining a national registry of appraisers who are certified and licensed by a state and who are also eligible to perform appraisals in federally related transactions; and (4) monitoring the practices, procedures, activities, and organizational structure of the Appraisal Foundation, a nonprofit educational corporation established by the appraisal industry in the United States.

Title V of the Housing and Economic Recovery Act of 2008 established the responsibility for the Federal banking agencies, through the FFIEC and in conjunction with the Farm Credit Administration, to develop and maintain a system for registering depository institution employees as registered loan originators with the Nationwide Mortgage Licensing System and Registry (NMLSR). The system shall at a minimum, furnish or cause to be furnished to the NMLSR information concerning the employees' identity, including: (A) fingerprints for submission to the Federal Bureau of Investigation and any governmental agency or entity authorized to receive such information for a State and national criminal history background check; and (B) personal history and experience, including authorization for the NMLSR to obtain information related to any administrative, civil or criminal findings by any governmental jurisdiction.

The Council has six members: a member of the Board of Governors of the Federal Reserve System appointed by the Chairman of the Board, the Chairman of the Federal Deposit Insurance Corporation, the Chairman of the Board of the National Credit Union Administration, the Comptroller of the Currency, the Director of the Office of Thrift Supervision, and the Chairman of the State Liaison Committee. To encourage the application of uniform examination principles and standards by the state and federal supervisory authorities, the Council established, in accordance with the requirement of the statute, an advisory State Liaison Committee. To effectively administer projects in all its functional areas, the Council established six interagency staff task forces, each of which includes one senior official from each of the member agencies:

- Consumer Compliance
- Examiner Education
- Information Sharing
- Reports
- Supervision
- Surveillance Systems

The Council also established the Legal Advisory Group, composed of the general or chief counsel of each of the member agencies, to provide support to the Council and staff in the substantive areas of concern;

and the Agency Liaison Group, composed of senior officials responsible for coordinating the efforts of their respective agencies' staff members. The task forces and the Legal Advisory Group provide research and analytical papers and proposals on the issues that the Council addresses.

Administration of the Council

The Council holds regular meetings at least twice a year. It holds other meetings whenever called by the Chairman or three or more Council members.

The Council's activities are funded in several ways. Most of the Council's funds are derived from assessments on its five federal member agencies. It receives tuition fees from non-agency attendees to cover some of the costs associated with its examiner education program. The Council also receives reimbursement for the services it provides to support preparation of the quarterly Uniform Bank Performance Report.

In 2008, the Federal Reserve Board provided budget and accounting services to the Council. The Council is supported by a small, full-time administrative staff in its operations office and in its examiner education program, which are located at the Council's examiner training facility in Arlington, Virginia. Each Council staff member is detailed from one of the five member agencies represented on the Council but is considered an employee of the Council.

Record of Council Activities

The Federal Financial Institutions Examination Council in Session.

The following section is a chronological record of the official actions taken by the FFIEC during 2008 pursuant to the Federal Financial Institutions Examination Council Act of 1978, as amended, and the Home Mortgage Disclosure Act (HMDA).

January 22, 2008

Action. Approved the posting of Senior Program Administrator positions with the possibility of making them permanent assignments.

Explanation. The Senior Program Administrator positions are filled by employees from each of the five federal member agencies. By providing permanent position opportunities the Examiner Education Office expects to reduce turnover.

March 5, 2008

Action. Approved the issuance of the Council's annual interagency awards.

Explanation. The Council has an interagency awards program that recognizes individuals of the member agencies who have provided outstanding service to the Council on interagency projects and programs during the previous year.

March 7, 2008

Action. Approved the appointment of six task force chairs.

Explanation. The chairs for all six standing task forces are approved annually and are drawn from management and staff of the five Federal member agencies.

March 27, 2008

Action. Approved the 2007 annual report of the Council to the Congress.

Explanation. The legislation establishing the Council requires that,

3

not later than April l of each year, the Council publish an annual report covering its activities during the preceding year.

March 27, 2008

Action. Accepted the annual external audit report.

Explanation. The Council is audited by an outside accounting firm annually. The audit report includes a review of the Council's financial statements as well as a report on internal controls and compliance with government accounting standards.

March 31, 2008

Action. Approved the change of the Chairman for the Task Force on Examiner Education.

Explanation. The Council has the authority to designate, upon recommendations received from the task force committees, a task force chairman from among the voting members of each of the permanent task force committees.

April 10, 2008

Action. Approved the Central Data Repository steering committee's request to award a Task Order 4 to address high priority enhancements.

Explanation. The Council is required to approve task orders that exceed a specific dollar amount.

Members of the Council Engaged in Discussions During the October 2008 Council Meeting.

May 29, 2008

Action. Approved the appointment of a new Executive Secretary.

Explanation. The Executive Secretary role is competitively filled by a candidate from one of the five federal member agencies of the FFIEC.

June 28, 2008

Action. Approved the revised Rules of Operation, Resolutions, and Task Force Charters documenting the role of the State Liaison Committee as a member of the FFIEC and each of the Task Forces.

Explanation. The Financial Services Regulatory Relief Act of 2006 made the Chairman of the State Liaison Committee a voting member of the council. The State Liaison Committee's involvement with the task forces enables state regulators to participate in substantive policy discussions on a broad range of important regulatory subjects.

December 2, 2008

Action. Approved the 2008 Council budget.

Explanation. The Council is required to approve the annual budget that funds the Council's staff, programs, and activities.

STATE LIAISON REPORT

State Liaison Committee (from the left to right) Sandra Branson (MO), Douglas Foster (TX), John Munn (NE), D. Eric McClure (MO), and Mick Thompson (OK).

The State Liaison Committee consists of five representatives of state regulatory agencies that supervise financial institutions. The representatives are appointed for two-year terms. A State Liaison Committee member may have his or her two-year term extended by the appointing organization for an additional, consecutive two-year term. Each year, the State Liaison Committee elects one of its members to serve as chair for twelve months. The Council elects two of the five members. The American Council of State Savings Supervisors, the Conference of State Bank Supervisors, and the National Association of State Credit Union Supervisors designate the other three members. A list of the State Liaison Committee members appears in Appendix D of this report.

The Financial Services Regulatory Relief Act of 2006 made the Chairman of the State Liaison Committee a voting member of the council. With the passage of this act, the State Liaison Committee appointed state supervisors to represent the state system on all task forces and working groups. The State Liaison Committee's involvement with such groups enables state regulators to participate in substantive policy discussions on a broad range of important regulatory subjects, reflecting the spirit and intent of Congress in establishing the State Liaison Committee. The Conference of State Bank Supervisors serves as the primary liaison to the FFIEC for all administrative matters.

ACTIVITIES OF THE INTERAGENCY STAFF TASK FORCES

Task Force on Consumer Compliance

The Task Force on Consumer Compliance promotes policy coordination, a common supervisory approach, and uniform enforcement of consumer protection laws and regulations. The task force identifies and analyzes emerging consumer compliance issues and develops proposed policies and procedures to foster consistency among the agencies. Additionally, the task force reviews legislation, regulations, and policies at the state and federal level that may have a bearing on the compliance responsibilities of the five federal member agencies.

During 2008, the task force used two standing subcommittees to help promote its mission: the Community Reinvestment Act (CRA) Subcommittee and the Home Mortgage Disclosure Act (HMDA)/CRA Data Collection Subcommittee. The task force also creates ad hoc working groups to handle particular projects and assignments. The task force meets monthly to address and resolve common issues in compliance supervision. While significant issues or recommendations are referred to the FFIEC for action, the FFIEC has delegated to the task force the authority to make certain decisions and recommendations.

Initiatives Addressed in 2008

CRA Subcommittee Activities

The Federal Reserve Board, the Office of the Comptroller of the Currency, the Office of Thrift Supervision and the Federal Deposit Insurance Corporation (the agencies) adjusted the asset thresholds, based on the consumer price index, for small- and intermediate-small banks.

The agencies adopted nine new and substantive changes to 14 existing interagency questions and answers on CRA in response to comments received to the revisions proposed in 2007. These questions and answers, published on January 6, 2009, consolidate and supersede all previously published interagency questions and answers. In addition, the agencies proposed two new and revised questions and answers. Comment on these proposed provisions are due by March 9, 2009.

HMDA/CRA Data Collection Subcommittee Activities

The HMDA and CRA Data Collection Subcommittee continued its efforts to update the systems that collect, process, and report HMDA and CRA data and began studying the implications of implementing data from Census Bureau's American Community Survey.

Delivery of Electronic Disclosures Examination Procedures

The task force approved revised procedures for Regulations M and Z to comply with the E-Sign Act and the agencies individually approved revised examination procedures for Regulations M and Z, to comply with the E-Sign Act.

Revise Regulation DD (Truth in Savings) Examination Procedures

The task force approved Regulation DD (Truth in Savings) examination procedures to comply with regulatory changes on electronic disclosures and to incorporate the GAO's recommendation related to institutions' provision of disclosure information on bank fees to consumers.

Task Force on Consumer Compliance meeting.

Interagency Fair Lending Examination Procedures

The task force updated interagency fair lending examination procedures, which included discrimination risk indicators for loan pricing, steering, and redlining, and a discussion of mortgage brokers and associated fair lending risks.

Reverse Mortgages

The task force established a working group to investigate practices in the reverse mortgage market. After reviewing data and interviewing external and internal stakeholders, the task force asked the working group to draft an appendix to the Truth in Lending procedures to address the total annual loan cost calculation, advertising and disclosure requirements for this product; and to develop examination guidance that would emphasize best practices to lenders.

Compliance Ratings Definitions

In 2006 the task force began developing and pilot testing a revised Uniform Interagency Consumer Compliance Rating System that will update the current compliance rating system and ensure that the banking agencies are implementing a system that is flexible enough for each agency to use as part of its individual exam approach. The task force approved the proposed updated compliance ratings definitions that will be published in the *Federal Register*, subject to agency approval.

Consumer Complaints

The working group developed a Consumer Help Center on the FFIEC's website with a search function to direct consumers to the appropriate regulator. In addition, the working group is developing a Statement of Work for the implementation of a centralized toll free number that consumers would use to contact the appropriate regulator.

Flood Insurance

The working group published and reviewed comments received on new and revised interagency Q&As regarding flood insurance. The working group has worked with FEMA and will submit a final draft of the Q&As to the task force in early 2009.

John Warner National Defense Authorization Act and Servicemembers' Civil Relief Act (SCRA)

The task force adopted examination procedures implementing the Talent-Nelson amendment to the John Warner National Defense Authorization Act. Examination procedures for the Servicemembers' Civil Relief Act (SCRA), which will reflect the changes to the SCRA made by the Housing and Economic Reform Act of 2008, are being drafted.

Fair Credit Reporting Act

The Fair Credit Reporting Act Examination Procedures working group developed procedures for Affiliate Marketing, Identity Theft Red Flags, and address discrepancies and rec-onciliation. The task force approved the "red flags" and address discrepancies/reconciliation procedures as well as the Affiliate Marketing procedures.

Regulation E

The task force approved examination procedures to comply with regulatory changes on electronic disclosures as well as other amendments to Regulation E.

Task Force on Examiner Education

The Task Force on Examiner Education is responsible for overseeing the FFIEC's examiner education program on behalf of the Council. The task force promotes interagency education through timely, cost-efficient, state-of-the-art training programs for agency examiners and staff. The task force develops programs on its own initiative and in response to requests from the Council or other Council task forces. Each fall, task force staff prepares a training calendar based on demand

Task Force on Examiner Education meeting.

from the five federal member agencies and state financial institution regulators. Based on this demand, task force staff schedules, delivers, and evaluates training programs throughout the year. In 2008, over 2,600 people attended task force-sponsored training (see the table below for details of participation by program and agency).

Initiatives Addressed in 2008

The Task Force on Examiner Education has continued to ensure that the FFIEC's educational programs meet the needs of agency personnel, are cost–effective, and are widely available. The task force meets monthly with the Examiner Education Office staff to discuss emerging topics, to review feedback from each course and conference, and to develop a framework for future conferences and courses. The solid partnership between the task force principals and the Examiner Education Office staff promotes open and regular communication which con-tinues to result in high quality, well-received training.

Specific accomplishments during 2008 include the completion of a standalone, CD-based training product for agency personnel regarding the Financial Analysis of Technology Service Providers. In addition, a well-received pilot session of a Commercial Real Estate Analysis for Financial Institution Examiners course allowed for this course to be added to the 2009 training calendar. The InfoBase architec-

2008 FFIEC Training by Agency and Sponsored—Actual, as of December 31, 2008

Event Name	FRB	FRB State Sponsored	FDIC	FDIC State Sponsored	NCUA	OCC	OTS	FCA	FHFB	Other	Total
Advanced BSA/AML Conference	35	17	35	28	11	31	15	0	1	15	188
Advanced Cash Flow Concepts & Analysis: Beyond	20	13	74	1	7	30	13	3	0	0	161
Advanced Commercial Credit Analysis	33	14	70	32	3	7	8	10	0	0	177
Anti-Money Laundering Workshop	53	32	53	21	16	0	28	0	0	12	215
Advanced Fraud Investigation Techniques for Examiners	8	5	8	0	1	3	1	0	0	0	26
Asset Management Forum	35	16	24	18	0	19	7	0	0	1	120
Capital Markets Conference	27	18	72	31	12	15	10	0	4	1	190
Capital Markets Specialists Conference	15	8	74	11	7	17	12	9	5	0	158
Cash Flow Construction and Analysis	24	21	35	32	3	16	12	3	0	1	147
Commercial Real Estate	3	0	4	0	6	5	4	0	0	0	22
Community Financial Institutions Lending Forum	18	7	53	11	3	13	14	1	2	0	122
Financial Crimes Seminar	43	34	55	21	14	0	32	2	2	13	216
Fraud Identification On-line Training	2	0	15	0	0	6	2	0	0	8	33
Fraud Investigations Symposium	0	0	0	0	0	0	0	0	0	0	0
FRB Fundamentals of Fraud	0	0	4	16	3	3	1	0	2	4	33
Information Technology Conference	60	11	46	7	20	39	25	11	2	0	221
Instructor Training School	41	4	6	0	4	15	1	2	0	2	75
International Banking School	8	1	3	1	2	2	4	0	0	0	21
International Banking (Self-Study)	5	0	8	0	0	6	2	0	0	9	30
Payment Systems Risk Conference	25	12	17	4	10	9	5	0	0	6	88
Real Estate Appraisal Review School	17	12	17	0	2	0	49	1	0	0	98
Real Estate Appraisal Review On-line	3	0	8	0	2	0	1	0	0	0	14
Supervisory Updates & Emerging Issues	71	46	41	23	4	29	32	6	9	2	263
Testifying School	0	0	14	1	0	11	0	0	0	0	26
Grand Total	**546**	**271**	**736**	**258**	**130**	**276**	**278**	**48**	**27**	**74**	**2,644**
Percentage	20.65	10.25	27.84	9.76	4.92	10.44	10.51	1.82	1.02	2.80	100
Combined Agency and Sponsored Percentage	30.90	NA	37.59	NA	4.92	10.44	10.51	1.82	1.02	2.80	100

ture implemented in 2001 continues to allow the FFIEC's Examiner Education Office to produce training and reference materials that can be delivered on CDs directly to all examiners concurrent with, or shortly after, the issuance of interagency statements, Council courses, or conferences. Updates to the new BSA/AML Examination Manual and the Information Technology Examination Handbook continue to be available to examiners and the industry through the FFIEC website: www.ffiec.gov.

Facilities

FFIEC rents office space, classrooms, and lodging facilities at the Federal Deposit Insurance Corporation's Seidman Center in Arlington, Virginia. This facility offers convenient access to two auditoriums and numerous classrooms.

Course Catalogue and Schedule

The course catalogue and schedule are available online at www.ffiec. gov/exam/education.htm.

Additionally, a printed copy of the 2009 course catalogue and schedule are available from the Examiner Education Office. To obtain a copy, contact:

Karen K. Smith, Manager
FFIEC Examiner Education Office
3501 Fairfax Drive
Room B-3030
Arlington, VA 22226-3550

Phone: (703) 516-5588

Task Force on Information Sharing

The Task Force on Information Sharing promotes the sharing of electronic information among FFIEC agencies in support of the supervision, regulation, and deposit insurance responsibilities of financial institution regulators. The task force provides a forum for FFIEC member agencies to discuss and address issues affecting the quality, consistency, efficiency, and security of interagency information sharing. Significant matters are referred, with recommendations, to the Council for action, and the task force has delegated authority from the Council to take certain actions.

To the extent possible, the agencies build on each other's information databases to minimize duplication of effort and promote consistency. The agencies participate in a program to share, in accordance with agency policy, electronic versions of their reports of examination, inspection reports, and other communications with financial institutions. The agencies also provide each other with access to their organizations' structure, financial, and supervisory information on their regulated entities. The task force and its working groups use a collaborative web site to share information among the FFIEC agencies. The task force maintains a "Data Exchange Summary" listing the data files exchanged among FFIEC agencies and a repository of communications and documents critical to information sharing.

The task force has established one working group to address technology-development issues and another working group to perform interagency reconciliation of financial institution structure data. In addition, the task force receives demonstrations and reports on agency, financial industry, and other FFIEC initiatives pertaining to technology development, including the production and development status of the interagency Central Data Repository.

Initiatives Addressed in 2008

Technology Issues

The mission of the task force is to identify and implement technologies to make the sharing of interagency data more efficient and to accommodate changes in agency databases and technologies. The task force's Technology Working Group meets monthly to develop technological solutions to common data-sharing issues among the agencies. The working group coordinates the automated transfer of data files among the agencies and suggests better and more efficient ways to share financial

Kenneth Kapner instructs at the FFIEC's Capital Markets Conference.

Task Force on Information Sharing meeting.

and supervisory data. The working group also maintains a Task Scope Matrix to identify and provide status reports on all outstanding work group projects and an inventory of possible future technology projects. In addition, the working group continues to develop necessary links and processes to exchange electronic documents and to store documents and critical materials on interagency information changes in the collaborative web site repository.

High-speed T1 communication lines linking the Federal Deposit Insurance Corporation, the Federal Reserve Board, and the Office of the Comptroller of the Currency have eliminated the use of magnetic tapes or disks for sharing electronic data among these agencies. Further research is being conducted to ensure efficiency of data utilization through the reduction of volume and duplication of efforts. New technologies are being implemented in improving data sharing.

In 2008, the working group continued to work on long-term projects related to the Federal Reserve Board's new bulk data transfer facility, National Information Center (NIC) Architecture Redesign Initia-

tive, and changes to NIC tables to implement the Structure Processing Application.

Completed projects included a secure, automated connection between the Federal Reserve Board and the National Credit Union Administration; a feed of Office of Thrift Supervision supervisory documents to the Federal Reserve Board via secure email; and end-to-end testing of the new Basel II data transfer between the Federal Reserve Board and other agencies. The next phase of Basel II testing will evaluate the data collection component.

Structure Data Reconciliation

The task force's Structure Data Reconciliation Working Group (SDRWG) continued to reconcile structure data about financial institutions regulated by FFIEC agencies to ensure that the information the agencies report is consistent and accurate. The SDRWG's quarterly reconcilements have greatly resolved data discrepancies among the agencies.

Task Force on Reports

The law establishing the Council

and defining its functions requires the Council to develop uniform reporting systems for federally supervised financial institutions and their holding companies and subsidiaries. To meet this objective, the Council established the Task Force on Reports. The task force helps to develop interagency uniformity in the reporting of periodic information that is needed for effective supervision and other public policy purposes. As a consequence, the task force is concerned with issues such as the development and interpretation of reporting instructions, including responding to inquiries about the instructions from reporting institutions and the public; the application of accounting standards to specific transactions; the development and application of processing standards; the monitoring of data quality; and the assessment of reporting burden. In addition, the task force works with other organizations, including the Securities and Exchange Commission, the Financial Accounting Standards Board, and the American Institute of Certified Public Accountants. The task force is also responsible for any special projects related to these subjects that the Council may assign. To help the task force carry out its responsibilities, working groups are organized as needed to handle specialized or technical accounting, reporting, instructional, and processing matters.

Initiatives Addressed in 2008

Reporting Requirements for the Consolidated Reports of Condition and Income and the Thrift Financial Report

In January 2008, the task force approved a final Paperwork Reduction Act (PRA) *Federal Register* notice on revisions to the Consolidated Reports of Condition and Income (Call Report) for banks, and one instructional change to both the Call Report and the Thrift Financial Report (TFR) for savings associations, that had been issued for public comment in September 2007. As proposed, these reporting changes were to take effect on March 31, 2008, and included adding new items related to 1-4 family residential mortgage lending, modifying the trading account definition in response to a new fair value option accounting standard, expanding the schedules for the trading account and fair value measurements, adding data items on loans not held for trading to which the fair value option is applied, and revising the threshold for reporting significant items of other noninterest income and expense. The instructional change for the two reports involved daily average deposit reporting by newly insured banks for deposit insurance assessment purposes. After considering the comments received, the task force agreed in December 2007 not to proceed with certain new fair value-related items and to make the reporting of several new Call Report items optional for the March 31, 2008, report date and required beginning June 30, 2008. The Federal Deposit Insurance Corporation (FDIC), the Federal Reserve Board (Board), the Office of the Comptroller of the Currency (OCC), and the Office of Thrift Supervision (OTS) (collectively, the agencies) published the final PRA notice on the revised reporting requirements in February 2008. The U.S. Office of Management and Budget (OMB) approved these revisions and their effective dates in March 2008.

The task force organized interagency working groups of subject matter experts in February 2008 to evaluate the need for possible revisions to data items currently collected in the Call Report and TFR and for new data items in three areas: securitizations, both for issuers and investors; mortgages, other loans, and credit risk; and trust and fiduciary activities. Another working group was charged with considering the information received in 2007 from a variety of user groups within the agencies and state super-

visory authorities on the usage of the data in the Call Report and the TFR to determine where burden-reducing revisions could be made. The task force received the working groups' recommendations in April 2008 and also considered revisions to the information currently reported on fair value measurements and certain other possible reporting changes. After extensive review and discussion of the full range of suggested revisions, the task force developed a condensed set of proposed revisions to the Call Report for implementation in three phases in March, June, and December 2009. The agreed-upon proposal reflected a thorough and careful review of the agencies' data needs as institutions experience the most turbulent economic environment in decades. The OTS incorporated several of the proposed Call Report revisions into a separate proposal for the TFR.

In September 2008, the task force approved, and the FDIC, the Board, and the OCC (the banking agencies) published, an initial PRA *Federal Register* notice requesting comment on the proposed Call Report revisions. The comment period for these proposed revisions ended November 24, 2008. After considering the comments received, the task force decided to move forward with most of the reporting changes, with limited modifications in response to certain comments, on the phased-in basis that had been proposed. The task force is continuing to evaluate a few of the proposed revisions in light of the comments received. Should they be implemented in some form after further evaluation, they would not take effect before December 2009.

On October 14, 2008, the FDIC announced the Temporary Liquidity Guarantee Program (TLGP), which has two primary components: the Debt Guarantee Program, by which the FDIC will guarantee the payment of certain newly issued senior unsecured debt, and the Transac-

tion Account Guarantee Program, by which the FDIC will guarantee certain noninterest-bearing transaction accounts. To enable the FDIC to calculate assessments for institutions participating in the Transaction Account Guarantee Program, the task force approved revisions to the Call Report, the TFR, and the Report of Assets and Liabilities of U.S. Branches and Agencies of Foreign Banks (FFIEC 002 report). An institution participating in the Transaction Account Guarantee Program would report the amount and number of its noninterest-bearing transaction accounts, as defined in the FDIC's TLGP regulations, of more than $250,000. On November 26, 2008, OMB approved the agencies' emergency clearance request seeking approval to collect these two data items beginning December 31, 2008. Because OMB's approval of the agencies' emergency clearance request expires in May 2009, the task force approved an initial PRA *Federal Register* notice in which the agencies propose under OMB's normal clearance procedures to collect these items in the Call Report, the TFR, and the FFIEC 002 report each quarter until the Transaction Account Guarantee Program ends. The agencies published the notice on December 23, 2008.

The task force conducted monthly interagency conference calls during 2008 to discuss Call Report instructional matters and related accounting issues to reach uniform interagency positions on these issues.

Central Data Repository (CDR)

During 2008, the agencies continued to devote significant staff resources to enhancing the CDR for processing the quarterly Call Reports filed by insured commercial banks and state-chartered savings banks.

The agencies expanded the options on its public data distribution web site to make Call Report data available more quickly and easily. The agencies also upgraded agency extract procedures and the data validation engine, improved the metadata management tool to reduce agency analyst workload and increase the efficiency of tasks, and improved usability, data import features, and data extract features.

The contractor and the agencies continued development of the Uniform Bank Performance Report (UBPR) within the CDR. This effort was originally scheduled for completion in 2008, but software development problems required a schedule revision. The new schedule shows completing the functionality for financial ratio management and calculation in June 2009 and implementing the functionality to make UBPR data available to agency users and the public in December 2009.

Other Activities

In December 2007, the task force approved regulatory capital reporting requirements associated with the implementation of the Advanced Capital Adequacy Framework (known as Basel II) and a final PRA *Federal Register* notice, which the agencies published in January 2008. These reporting requirements were developed by an interagency Data Collection Group (DCG) of subject matter experts and originally had been issued for comment as the proposed FFIEC 101 report in September 2006. The revisions to this proposed report, which the DCG made during 2007 to address commenters' concerns about reporting burden and their questions about the reporting requirements, included eliminating three schedules and several hundred reportable data items, lengthening the submission period for the report during an institution's parallel run period, and allowing more data items to be reported on an optional basis. Other changes to the proposed reporting requirements and instructions were made in response to changes the banking agencies incorporated in their final rules for the Advanced Capital Adequacy Framework.

The agencies received four comment letters on the final PRA notice for the FFIEC 101 report. In general, commenters sought clarification on, or made recommendations pertaining to, various technical aspects of the reporting requirements. At OMB's request, the DCG drafted a paper describing the disposition of the comments that would be sent to commenters under cover of a letter from the task force. After obtaining approval from the agencies' senior managements, the task force sent the cover letter and discussion paper to the commenters and OMB in May 2008. OMB approved the FFIEC 101 reporting requirements.

In January 2008, the task force approved, and the Board published, an initial PRA *Federal Register* notice requesting comment on proposed revisions to the FFIEC 002 report for implementation in June 2008. These revisions incorporated certain changes into the FFIEC 002 report that were previously made to the bank Call Report with respect to data on real estate loans, credit derivatives, fair value measurements, and, for FDIC-insured branches, the deposit insurance assessment base. In response to comments, the task force made no modifications to the proposal, but agreed to delay implementation to September 30, 2008, except for the deposit insurance-related changes for which a transition period was to begin June 30, 2008. In March 2008, the task force approved, and the Board published, a final PRA *Federal Register* notice requesting comment on the reporting changes and modified implementation schedule. OMB approved the changes and implementation schedule in June 2008.

Task Force on Supervision

The Task Force on Supervision coordinates and oversees matters relating to safety-and-soundness supervision and examination of depository institutions. It provides a forum for the member agencies

to promote quality, consistency, and effectiveness in examination and supervisory practices and to reduce unnecessary regulatory burden. While significant issues are referred, with recommendations, to the Council for action, the Council has delegated to the task force the authority to make certain decisions and recommendations, provided all task force members agree. Meetings are held regularly to address and resolve common supervisory issues. The task force has also established and maintains supervisory communication protocols to be used in emergencies. These protocols are periodically tested through table-top exercises with task force members and key supervisory personnel.

The task force has three standing subcommittees:

- The *Capital Subcommittee* serves as a forum for senior policy staff members to discuss various initiatives pertaining to the agencies' regulatory capital standards.

- The *Information Technology (IT) Subcommittee* serves as a forum to address information systems and technology issues as they relate to financial institutions. The IT Subcommittee oversees and administers the FFIEC's Technology Service Provider (TSP) Examination and Shared Application Software Review (SASR) programs. Through the FFIEC'S Multi-Regional Data Processing Servicer program, the agencies conduct joint information technology examinations of the largest, systemically important TSPs and other entities that provide critical banking services. The SASR program provides a mechanism for the agencies to review and share information on mission-critical software applications, such as loans, deposits, general ledger systems, and other critical software tools that are used by a large number of financial institutions. These programs help the agencies identify potential systemic risks and provide examiners with information that can reduce time and resources needed to examine the IT-related processing software and external services at user financial institutions.

- The *Bank Secrecy Act/Anti-Money Laundering (BSA/AML) Working Group* seeks to enhance coordination of BSA/AML training, guidance, and policy. The coordination includes continuing communication between federal and state banking agencies and the Financial Crimes Enforcement Network. The BSA/AML Working Group builds on existing efforts and works to strengthen the activities that are already being pursued by other formal and informal interagency groups providing oversight of various BSA/AML matters. BSA/AML training, guidance, and policy includes: (1) procedures and resource materials for examination purposes; (2) joint examiner training related to the Manual; (3) outreach to the banking industry on BSA/AML policy matters; and (4) other issues related to consistency of BSA/AML supervision.

The task force also establishes ad hoc working groups to handle individual projects and assignments, as needed.

Initiatives Addressed in 2008

Pandemic Guidance

The task force's pandemic working group engaged in several projects designed to help the agencies plan and prepare for supervisory efforts that may be needed during a pandemic event. The working group sponsored a Roundtable on Pandemic Planning, which had approximately 170 industry attendees, including some international participants. The FFIEC's "Business Continuity Planning" booklet of the *Information Technology Handbook* series was updated in March 2008 to include guidance on identifying the continuity planning that should

be in place to minimize the potential adverse effects of a pandemic event. The working group also engaged in dialogue with the industry regarding potential needs for regulatory relief in the event of a pandemic. An emergency preparedness, response, and recovery meeting was held in March 2008 among the FFIEC members and industry trade group representatives. A second meeting was held in September 2008.

Information Technology

Financial institutions' significant use of information technology services, whether generated internally or obtained from third-party service providers, contributes to their operational risk environment in general and their data security risk in particular. A major effort of the Information Technology subcommittee and agencies is continually maintaining the FFIEC Information Technology handbook, which was first published in 1996. The handbook now consists of a series of topical booklets addressing issues such as business continuity planning, information security, and electronic banking.

The Information Technology Subcommittee, in conjunction with the Task Force on Examiner Education, sponsors an annual Information Technology conference for the agencies' examination staff to explore emerging risks and industry best practices.

Capital Standards

Although each of the four federal banking agencies has its own capital regulations, the task force's standing Capital Subcommittee and several of its working groups often coordinate efforts among the agencies to promote joint issuance of capital rules and related interpretive guidance, thereby minimizing interagency differences and reducing the potential burden on the banking industry. A major focus of the federal banking agencies has been the development of the advanced capital adequacy

framework (Basel II) and potentially a standardized Basel II framework.

BSA/AML Working Group

The BSA/AML working group sponsored its second FFIEC BSA/AML Advanced Specialists Conference in October 2008. Feedback from the conference was positive. The BSA/AML working group continued to solicit feedback from the banking industry and examination staff in order to revise the BSA/AML examination manual in 2009. The planned revision will clarify supervisory expectations and incorporate regulatory changes since the manual's first release in 2005. The agencies continued to share information with the Financial Crimes Enforcement Network and with the Office of Foreign Assets Control.

Task Force on Surveillance Systems

The Task Force on Surveillance Systems oversees the development and implementation of uniform interagency surveillance and monitoring systems. It provides a forum for the member agencies to discuss best practices to be used in those systems and to consider the development of new financial analysis tools. The task force's principal objective has been to develop and produce the Uniform Bank Performance Report (UBPR). UBPRs present financial statistics and peer group comparisons of individual banks for current and historical periods. These reports are important tools for completing supervisory evaluations of a bank's condition and performance, as well as for planning onsite examinations. The banking agencies also use the data from these reports in their automated monitoring systems to identify potential or emerging problems in insured banks.

UBPRs are produced for each commercial bank and insured savings bank in the United States that is supervised by the Federal Reserve Board, the Federal Deposit Insur-

Task Force on Surveillance Systems meeting.

ance Corporation, or the Office of the Comptroller of the Currency. UBPR data are also available to all state bank supervisors. While the UBPR is principally designed to meet the examination and surveillance needs of the federal and state banking agencies, the task force also makes UBPRs available to banks and the public through a public web site; www.ffiec.gov.

Initiatives Addressed in 2008

UBPR Peer Group Information Available Faster

The task force implemented a new process that allows UBPR Peer Group data to be published once all banks have filed their Call Report. With these changes, peer group data will be available shortly after the filing date of the applicable Call Report form.

Loan Yield Data Improved

The task force expanded loan yield information shown in the UBPR by taking advantage of new data in single family loans and other real estate loans. Data for the bank as well as peer group averages and percentile

rankings were added to the UBPR. It is anticipated that this new information will provide added insight into the contribution of real estate loans to bank profitability.

Loan Delinquency Data Improved

The task force expanded information for restructured real estate loans and loans in foreclosure in the UBPR by taking advantage of new data in the Call Report. New dollar, ratio, peer group average, and percentile ranking data were added to the UBPR. This new data should provide more information about bank loan quality.

UBPR Delivered to a Wide Audience

UBPR for December 31, 2007; March 31, 2008; June 30, 2008; and September 30, 2008 was produced and delivered during 2008 to federal and state banking agencies. Additionally, the UBPR website was utilized to deliver the same data to bankers and the general public. The task force strives to deliver the most up-to-date UBPR data to all users. Thus UBPR data is updated at a minimum of once a week and more frequently during the time when new Call Report data is being submitted by banks.

Enhancements Planned to the UBPR

In 2009, the task force plans several enhancements to the UBPR that will take advantage of new and existing Call Report data. Included in those changes will be publication of income and expense data for fiduciary activities. The task force will continue to work closely with the Task Force on Reports and the Central Data Repository (CDR) Steering Committee in implementing a move of UBPR processing to the CDR.

Information Available on the UBPR Web Site

UBPR Availability

To provide broad public access to information about the financial condition of insured banks, the task force publishes a final quarterly version of the UBPR for each institution, typically within fifteen to twenty days of the Call Report due date. Additionally, early UBPR data is typically available fifteen days before the Call Report filing date. Bankers and the general public may access these reports on the FFIEC web site at no charge. In addition to publishing current reports, the task force regularly refreshes all historic UBPR data on the web site.

Other UBPR Reports

Several web-based statistical reports supporting UBPR analysis are also updated on the web site. These reports (1) summarize the performance of each of the UBPR's peer groups (determined by size, location, and business line), (2) detail the distribution of UBPR performance ratios for banks in each of these peer groups, (3) list the individual banks included in each peer group, and (4) compare a bank to the performance of a user-defined custom peer group.

Custom Peer Group Tool

The Custom Peer allows bankers, bank supervisors, and the general public to create custom peer groups based on financial and geographical criteria and to display all UBPR pages with peer group statistics and percentile rankings derived from a custom peer group.

Please visit http://www.ffiec.gov/UBPR.htm for additional information about the UBPR, including distribution schedules, descriptions of pending changes, and instructions on using online UBPR tools. Standardized UBPR quarterly data in delimited files on DVD is also available for $400. Information on ordering items may be obtained by calling (703) 516-1071, sending an e-mail message to FFIEC_UBPR@fdic.gov or writing the Council at:

Federal Financial Institutions
  Examination Council
3501 Fairfax Drive, Room D8073a
Arlington, VA 22226-3550

The five federal financial institution regulatory agencies represented on the Council have primary federal supervisory jurisdiction over 16,342 domestically chartered banks, thrift institutions, and credit unions. On December 31, 2008, these financial institutions held total assets of more than $16.6 trillion. The Board of Governors of the Federal Reserve System and the Office of Thrift Supervision also have primary federal supervisory responsibility for commercial bank holding companies and for savings and loan holding companies, respectively.

Three banking agencies on the Council have authority to oversee the operations of U.S. branches and agencies of foreign banks. The International Banking Act of 1978 (IBA) authorizes the Office of the Comptroller of the Currency to license federal branches and agencies of foreign banks and permits U.S. branches that accept only wholesale deposits to apply for insurance with the Federal Deposit Insurance Corporation. According to the Federal Deposit Insurance Corporation Improvement Act of 1991 (FDICIA), foreign banks that wish to operate insured entities in the United States and accept retail deposits must organize under separate U.S. charters. Existing insured retail branches may continue to operate as branches. The IBA also subjects those U.S. offices of foreign banks to many provisions of the Federal Reserve Act and the Bank Holding Company Act. The IBA gives primary examining authority to the Office of the Comptroller of the Currency, the Federal Deposit Insurance Corporation, and various state authorities for the offices within their jurisdictions and gives the Federal Reserve Board residual examining authority over all U.S. banking operations of foreign banks.

Board of Governors of the Federal Reserve System

The Federal Reserve Board was established in 1913. It is headed by a seven-member Board of Governors, each member of which is appointed by the President, with the advice and consent of the Senate, for a fourteen-year term. Subject to confirmation by the Senate, the President selects two Board members to serve four-year terms as Chairman and Vice Chairman. The Federal Reserve Board's activities that are most relevant to the work of the Council are the following:

- examining, supervising, and regulating state member banks (that is, state-chartered banks that are members of the Federal Reserve System); bank holding companies; Edge Act and agreement corporations; and, in conjunction with the licensing authorities, the U.S. offices of foreign banks;

- developing and issuing regulations, policies, and guidance applicable to organizations within the Federal Reserve Board's supervisory oversight authority; and

- approving or denying applications for mergers, acquisitions, and changes in control by state member banks and bank holding companies, applications for foreign operations of member banks and Edge Act and agreement corporations, and applications by foreign banks to establish or acquire U.S. banks and to establish U.S. branches, agencies, or representative offices.

Other supervisory and regulatory responsibilities of the Federal Reserve Board include regulating margin requirements on securities transactions, implementing certain statutes that protect consumers in credit and deposit transactions, monitoring compliance with other statutes (for example, the money-laundering provisions of the Bank Secrecy Act), and regulating transactions between banking affiliates.

Policy decisions are implemented by the Federal Reserve Board and the twelve Federal Reserve Banks, each of which has operational responsibility within a specific geographical area. The twelve Reserve Bank Districts are headquartered in Boston, New York, Philadelphia, Cleveland, Richmond, Atlanta, Chicago, St. Louis, Minneapolis, Kansas City, Dallas, and San Francisco. Each Reserve Bank has a president and other officers. Among other responsibilities, a Reserve Bank employs a staff of bank examiners who examine state member banks and Edge Act and agreement corporations, inspect bank holding companies, and examine the offices of foreign banks located within the Reserve Bank's District.

National banks, which must be members of the Federal Reserve, are chartered, regulated, and supervised by the Office of the Comptroller of the Currency. State-chartered banks may apply to and be accepted for membership in the Federal Reserve System, after which they are subject to the supervision and regulation of the Federal Reserve Board. Insured state-chartered banks that are not members of the Federal Reserve System are regulated and supervised by the Federal Deposit Insurance Corporation. The Federal Reserve Board has overall responsibility for foreign banking operations, including both U.S. banks operating abroad and foreign banks operating branches in the United States.

The Federal Reserve Board covers the expenses of its operations with revenue it generates principally from assessments on the twelve Federal Reserve Banks.

Federal Deposit Insurance Corporation

Congress created the Federal Deposit Insurance Corporation in 1933 with a mission to insure bank deposits and reduce the economic disruptions caused by bank failures. Management of the Federal Deposit Insurance Corporation is vested in a five-member Board of Directors. Three of the directors are directly appointed by the President, with the advice and consent of the Senate, for six-year terms. One of the three directors is designated by the President as Chairman for a term of five years, and another is designated as Vice Chairman. The other two Board members are the Comptroller of the Currency and the Director of the Office of Thrift Supervision. No more than three board members may be of the same political party.

The Federal Deposit Insurance Corporation's supervisory activities are conducted by the Division of Supervision and Consumer Protection. The division is organized into six regional offices and two area offices. The regional offices are located in Atlanta, Chicago, Dallas, Kansas City, New York, and San Francisco. The two area offices are located in Boston (reports to New York) and Memphis (reports to Dallas). In addition to the regional and area offices, the Federal Deposit Insurance Corporation maintains fifty-two field territory offices for risk management and thirty-two field territory offices for compliance, with dedicated examiners assigned to the four largest financial institutions. Bank liquidations are handled by the Division of Resolutions and Receiverships.

The Federal Deposit Insurance Corporation insures deposits at all insured commercial banks and savings institutions. On October 3, 2008, then President George W. Bush signed the Emergency Economic Stabilization Act of 2008, which tem-

porarily raises the basic limit on federal deposit insurance coverage from $100,000 to $250,000 per depositor. The temporary increase in deposit insurance coverage became effective upon the President's signature. The legislation provides that the basic deposit insurance limit will return to $100,000 after December 31, 2009.

The Federal Deposit Insurance Corporation's Board of Directors also approved regulatory changes to simplify the deposit insurance rules in 2008—the rules for determining the coverage available on revocable trust accounts, the calculation of deposit insurance coverage if five or fewer beneficiaries are named under a revocable trust agreement, and the deposit insurance rules for accounts held at FDIC-insured institutions by mortgage servicers. The Federal Deposit Insurance Corporation's Board of Directors also approved temporary deposit insurance changes under the Temporary Liquidity Guarantee Program (TLGP) allowing for unlimited coverage for non-interest transaction accounts offered by banks participating in the program. The TLGP also provided the Federal Deposit Insurance Corporation's guarantee of certain newly issued senior unsecured debt. The TLGP was announced by the Federal Deposit Insurance Corporation on October 14, 2008, as an initiative to counter the existing system-wide crisis in the nation's financial sector.

Assessments are collected by the Deposit Insurance Fund which the Federal Deposit Insurance Corporation oversees and manages. Recent bank failures significantly increased the Deposit Insurance Fund's losses, resulting in a decline in the reserve ratio. As of September 30, 2008, the reserve ratio stood at 0.76 percent, down from 1.01 percent at June 30, and 1.19 percent at March 31. The Federal Deposit Insurance Reform Act of 2005 requires that the Federal Deposit Insurance Corporation's Board of Directors adopt a restoration plan when the Deposit Insurance Fund designated reserve

ratio falls below 1.15 percent or is expected to within six months. Absent extraordinary circumstances, the restoration plan must provide that the reserve ratio increase to at least 1.15 percent no later than five years after the plan's establishment. The Federal Deposit Insurance Corporation's Board adopted a restoration plan on October 7, 2008.

Any depository institution that receives deposits may be insured by the Federal Deposit Insurance Corporation after application to and examination and approval by the Federal Deposit Insurance Corporation. After considering the (1) applicant's financial history and condition, (2) adequacy of the capital structure, (3) future earnings prospects, (4) general character of the management, (5) risk presented to the insurance fund, (6) convenience and needs of the community to be served, and (7) consistency of corporate powers, the Federal Deposit Insurance Corporation may approve or deny an application for insurance. The Federal Deposit Insurance Corporation Improvement Act of 1991 (FDICIA) expanded the Federal Deposit Insurance Corporation's approval authority to include national banks, all state-chartered banks that are members of the Federal Reserve System, and federal and state-chartered savings associations.

The Federal Deposit Insurance Corporation has primary federal regulatory and supervisory authority over insured state-chartered banks that are not members of the Federal Reserve System, and it has the authority to examine for insurance purposes any insured financial institution, either directly or in cooperation with state or other federal supervisory authorities. The FDICIA gives the Federal Deposit Insurance Corporation backup enforcement authority over all insured institutions; that is, the Federal Deposit Insurance Corporation can recommend that the appropriate federal agency take action against an insured institution and may do so itself if deemed necessary.

In protecting insured deposits, the Federal Deposit Insurance Corporation is charged with resolving the problems of insured depository institutions at the least possible cost to the deposit insurance fund. In carrying out this responsibility the Federal Deposit Insurance Corporation engages in several activities, including paying off deposits, arranging the purchase of assets and assumption of liabilities of failed institutions, effecting insured deposit transfers between institutions, creating and operating temporary bridge banks until a resolution can be accomplished, and using its conservatorship powers.

National Credit Union Administration

The National Credit Union Administration, established by the Federal Credit Union Act (Section 1752a) of Congress in 1934, is the agency that supervises the nation's federal credit union system. A three-member bipartisan board appointed by the President for six-year terms manages the National Credit Union Administration. The President also selects a member to serve as Chair of the board.

The main responsibilities of the National Credit Union Administration are the following:

• charter, examine, and supervise more than 4,900 federal credit unions nationwide;

• administer the National Credit Union Share Insurance Fund (NCUSIF), which insures member share accounts in more than 7,900 U.S. federal and state-chartered credit unions; and

• manage the Central Liquidity Facility, a central bank for credit unions, which provides liquidity to the credit union system.

The National Credit Union Administration also has statutory authority to examine and supervise NCUSIF-insured, state-chartered credit unions in coordination with state agencies.

The National Credit Union Administration has five regional offices across the United States that administer its responsibility to charter and supervise credit unions. Its examiners conduct on-site examinations and supervision of each federal credit union and selected state-chartered credit unions. The National Credit Union Administration is funded by the credit unions it regulates and insures.

Office of the Comptroller of the Currency

The Office of the Comptroller of the Currency is the oldest federal bank regulatory agency, established as a bureau of the Treasury Department by the National Currency Act of 1863. It is headed by the Comptroller of the Currency, who is appointed to a five-year term by the President with the advice and consent of the Senate. The Comptroller is also a Director of the FDIC and a Director of the Neighborhood Reinvestment Corporation.

The Office of the Comptroller of the Currency was created by Congress to charter, regulate, and supervise national banks. The Office of the Comptroller of the Currency regulates and supervises approximately 1,605 national banks and trust companies and 50 federal branches of foreign banks in the United States, accounting for about 69 percent of the total assets of all U.S. commercial banks and branches of foreign banks as of December 31, 2008.

The Office of the Comptroller of the Currency seeks to ensure a banking system in which national banks soundly manage their risks, comply with applicable laws, compete effectively with other providers of financial services, offer products and services that meet the needs of customers, and provide fair access to financial services and fair treatment of their customers. The Office of the

Comptroller of the Currency's mission-critical programs include:

• Chartering national banks and issuing interpretations related to permissible banking activities.

• Establishing and communicating regulations, policies, and operating guidance applicable to national banks.

• Supervising the national banking system through on-site examinations, off-site monitoring, systemic risk analyses, and appropriate enforcement activities.

To meet its objectives, the Office of the Comptroller of the Currency maintains a nationwide staff of bank examiners and other professional and support personnel. Headquartered in Washington, D.C., the Office of the Comptroller of the Currency has four district offices in Chicago, Dallas, Denver, and New York. In addition, the Office of the Comptroller of the Currency maintains a network of 44 field offices and 24 satellite locations in cities throughout the United States, as well as resident examiner teams in the 20 largest national banking companies and an examining office in London, England.

The Comptroller receives advice on policy and operational issues from an Executive Committee, comprised of senior agency officials who lead major business units.

The Office of the Comptroller of the Currency is funded primarily by semiannual assessments on national banks, interest revenue from its investment in U.S. Treasury securities, and other fees. The Office of the Comptroller of the Currency does not receive congressional appropriations for any of its operations.

Office of Thrift Supervision

The Office of Thrift Supervision was established as a bureau of the U. S. Department of the Treasury in 1989. The Office of Thrift Supervision charters and is the primary regulator for all federal savings associations, and shares joint responsibility with state authorities for supervision of all state savings associations. The Office of Thrift Supervision is also the primary regulator for all savings and loan holding companies, and has been affirmed by the European Union to be the consolidated, coordinating regulator for specific holding companies conducting operations in Europe.

The mission of the Office of Thrift Supervision is to supervise savings associations and their holding companies in order to maintain their safety and soundness and compliance with consumer laws, and to encourage a competitive industry that meets America's financial service needs.

The Office of Thrift Supervision carries out its mission by (1) adopting regulations governing the thrift institution industry, (2) examining and supervising savings associations and their affiliates, (3) taking appropriate action to enforce compliance with federal laws and regulations, and (4) acting on applications to charter or acquire a savings association. The Office of Thrift Supervision also has the authority to regulate, examine, supervise, and take enforcement action against savings and loan holding companies and other affiliates, as well as entities that provide services to savings associations.

The Office of Thrift Supervision is headed by a Director appointed by the President, with the advice and consent of the Senate, to serve a five-year term. The Director determines policy for the Office of Thrift Supervision and makes final decisions on regulations governing the industry as a whole and on measures affecting individual institutions. The Director also serves as a Director of the Federal Deposit Insurance Corporation and as a Director of the Neighborhood Reinvestment Corporation.

The agency conducts its operations from its headquarters in Washington, D.C., and five regional offices located in Jersey City, New Jersey (Northeast Region); Atlanta, Georgia (Southeast Region); Chicago, Illinois (Central Region); Dallas, Texas (Midwest Region); and Daly City, California (West Region).

The Office of Thrift Supervision uses no congressional appropriations to fund any of its operations. It draws its revenues primarily through fees and assessments levied on the institutions it regulates.

ASSETS, LIABILITIES, AND NET WORTH of U.S. Commercial Banks, Thrift Institutions and Credit Unions as of December 31, 2008[1]

Billions of dollars

Item	Total	U.S. Commercial Banks[2] National	State Member	State Non-Member	U.S. Branches and Agencies of Foreign Banks[5]	Thrift Institutions OTS-Regulated[4] Federal Charter	State Charter	Other FDIC-Supervised Savings Banks	Credit Unions[3] Federal Charter	State Charter
Total assets	**16,684**	**8,479**	**1,853**	**1,980**	**2,057**	**1,187**	**12**	**303**	**448**	**365**
Total loans and receivables (net)	8,857	4,425	915	1,339	617	794	8	198	307	254
Loans secured by real estate[6]	5,034	2,364	563	913	43	665	8	174	163	141
Consumer loans[7]	1,340	769	62	164	0	80	0	8	145	112
Commercial and industrial loans	1,868	988	211	219	365	63	0	16	2	4
All other loans and lease receivables[8]	793	417	97	68	209	0	0	2	0	0
LESS: Allowance for possible loan and lease losses	178	113	18	25	0	14	0	2	3	3
Federal funds sold and securities purchased under agreements to resell	791	581	77	30	68	29	0	5	0	1
Cash and due from depository institutions[9]	1,503	659	271	111	293	51	1	10	59	48
Securities and other obligations[10]	2,367	1,121	287	338	222	224	2	66	62	45
U.S. government obligations[11]	504	70	52	80	34	130	2	52	50	34
Obligations of state and local governments[12]	151	70	25	49	0	4	0	3	0	0
Other securities	1,712	981	210	209	188	90	0	11	12	11
Other assets[13]	3,166	1,693	303	162	857	89	1	24	20	17
Total liabilities	**15,291**	**7,699**	**1,674**	**1,777**	**2,057**	**1,079**	**10**	**270**	**399**	**326**
Total deposits and shares[14]	10,667	5,370	1,235	1,475	965	723	9	209	373	308
Federal funds purchased and securities sold under agreements to repurchase	1,036	648	87	68	155	65	0	12	1	0
Other borrowings[15]	2,277	1,057	202	197	467	270	1	46	22	15
Other liabilities[16]	1,311	624	150	37	470	21	0	3	3	3
Net worth[17]	**1,393**	**780**	**179**	**203**	**1**	**108**	**1**	**33**	**49**	**39**
Memorandum: Number of institutions reporting	16,342	1,534	848	4,687	247	743	67	410	4,847	2,959

Footnotes to Tables

1. The table covers institutions, including those in Puerto Rico and U.S. territories and possessions, insured by the Federal Deposit Insurance Corporation or National Credit Union Savings Insurance Fund. All branches and agencies of foreign banks in the United States, but excluding any in Puerto Rico and U.S. territories and possessions, are covered whether or not insured. Excludes Edge Act and agreement corporations that are not subsidiaries of U.S. commercial banks.

2. Reflects fully consolidated statements of FDIC-insured U.S. banks—including their foreign branches, foreign subsidiaries, branches in Puerto Rico and U.S. territories and possessions, and FDIC insured banks in Puerto Rico and U.S. territories and possessions. Excludes bank holding companies.

3. Data are for federally insured natural person credit unions only.

4. Data for thrift institutions regulated by the OTS reflects fully consolidated statements of condition and operations. Data for OTS regulated thrifts owned directly by other thrifts are excluded to avoid double counting results already included in the parents' financial statements.

5. These institutions are not required to file reports of income.

6. Includes loans secured by residential property, commercial property, farmland (including improvements) and unim-proved land; and construction loans secured by real estate.

7. Includes loans, except those secured by real estate, to individuals for household, family, and other personal expenditures including both installment and single payment loans. Net of unearned income on installment loans.

8. Includes loans to financial institutions, for purchasing or carrying securities, to finance agricultural production and other loans to farmers (except those secured by real estate), to states and political subdivisions and public authorities, and miscellaneous types of loans.

Notes continue on the next page

INCOME AND EXPENSES of U.S. Commercial Banks and Thrift Institutions for Twelve Months Ending December 31, 2008[1]

Billions of dollars

Item	Total	U.S. Commercial Banks[2]			Thrift Institutions			Credit Unions[3]	
					OTS-Regulated[4]		Other FDIC-Supervised Savings Banks		
		National	State Member	State Non-Member	Federal Charter	State Charter		Federal Charter	State Charter
Operating income	887	481	107	135	93	0	17	30	24
Interest and fees on loans	502	252	53	89	60	0	12	20	16
Other interest and dividend income	158	95	20	19	14	0	3	4	3
All other operating income	225	133	34	26	19	0	2	6	5
Operating expenses	863	451	107	126	112	0	16	28	23
Salaries and benefits	168	90	24	24	14	0	3	7	6
Interest on deposits and shares	186	86	22	35	22	0	5	9	7
Interest on other borrowed money	86	50	8	9	14	0	3	1	1
Provision for loan and lease losses	198	110	18	23	39	0	1	4	3
All other operating expenses	224	115	35	34	23	0	4	7	6
Net operating income	24	30	0	9	-19	0	1	2	1
Securities gains and losses	-14	-3	-1	-9	0	0	-1	0	0
Extraordinary Items	6	6	0	0	0	0	0	0	0
Income taxes	2	6	2	0	-6	0	0	0	0
Net income	14	27	-3	0	-13	0	0	2	1
Memorandum: Number of institutions reporting	16,095	1,534	848	4,687	743	67	410	4,847	2,959

9. Includes vault cash, cash items in process of collection, and balances with U.S. and foreign banks and other depository institutions (including demand and time deposits and certificates of deposit for all categories of institutions).

10. Includes government and corporate securities, including mortgage-backed securities and obligations of states and political subdivisions and of U.S. government agencies and corporations.

11. U.S. Treasury securities and securities of, and loans to, U.S. government agencies and corporations.

12. Securities issued by states and political subdivisions and public authorities, except for savings and loan associations and U.S. branches and agencies of foreign banks that do not report these securities separately. Loans to states and political subdivisions and public authorities are included in "All other loans and lease receivables."

13. Customers' liabilities on acceptances, real property owned, various accrual accounts, and miscellaneous assets. For U.S. branches and agencies of foreign banks, also includes net due from head office and other related institutions. For SAIF-insured institutions, also includes equity investment in service corporation subsidiaries.

14. Includes demand, savings, and time deposits, (including certificates of deposit at commercial banks, U.S. branches and agencies of foreign banks, and savings banks), credit balances at U.S. agencies of foreign banks and share balances at savings and loan associations and credit unions (including certificates of deposit, NOW accounts, and share draft accounts). For U.S. commercial banks, includes deposits in foreign offices, branches in U.S. territories and possessions, and Edge Act and Agreement corporation subsidiaries.

15. Includes interest-bearing demand notes issued to the U.S. Treasury, borrowing from Federal Reserve Banks and Federal Home Loan Banks, subordinated debt, limited life preferred stock, and other nondeposit borrowing.

16. Includes depository institutions' own mortgage borrowing, liability for capitalized leases, liability on acceptances executed, various accrual accounts, and miscellaneous liabilities. For U.S. branches and agencies of foreign banks, also includes net owed to head office and other related institutions.

17. Includes capital stock, surplus, capital reserves, and undivided profits.

NOTE: Data are rounded to nearest billion. Consequently, some information may not reconcile precisely. Additionally, balances less than $500 million will show as zero.

APPENDIX A: RELEVANT STATUTES

Federal Financial Institutions Examination Council Act

12 U.S.C. § 3301. Declaration of purpose

It is the purpose of this chapter to establish a Financial Institutions Examination Council which shall prescribe uniform principles and standards for the Federal examination of financial institutions by the Office of the Comptroller of the Currency, the Federal Deposit Insurance Corporation, the Board of Governors of the Federal Reserve System, the Federal Home Loan Bank Board, and the National Credit Union Administration and make recommendations to promote uniformity in the supervision of these financial institutions. The Council's actions shall be designed to promote consistency in such examination and to insure progressive and vigilant supervision.

12 U.S.C. § 3302. Definitions

As used in this chapter—

(1) the term "Federal financial institutions regulatory agencies" means the Office of the Comptroller of the Currency, the Board of Governors of the Federal Reserve System, the Federal Deposit Insurance Corporation, the Office of Thrift Supervision, and the National Credit Union Administration;

(2) the term "Council" means the Financial Institutions Examination Council; and

(3) the term "financial institution" means a commercial bank, a savings bank, a trust company, a savings association, a building and loan association, a homestead association, a cooperative bank, or a credit union.

12 U.S.C. § 3303. Financial Institutions Examination Council

(a) Establishment; composition

There is established the Financial Institutions Examination Council which shall consist of—

(1) the Comptroller of the Currency,

(2) the Chairman of the Board of Directors of the Federal Deposit Insurance Corporation,

(3) a Governor of the Board of Governors of the Federal Reserve System designated by the Chairman of the Board,

(4) the Director, Office of Thrift Supervision,

(5) the Chairman of the National Credit Union Administration Board; and

(6) the Chairman of the State Liaison Committee

(b) Chairmanship

The members of the Council shall select the first chairman of the Council. Thereafter the chairmanship shall rotate among the members of the Council.

(c) Term of office

The term of the Chairman of the Council shall be two years.

(d) Designation of officers and employees

The members of the Council may, from time to time, designate other officers or employees of their respective agencies to carry out their duties on the Council.

(e) Compensation and expenses

Each member of the Council shall serve without additional compensation but shall be entitled to reasonable expenses incurred while carrying out his official duties as such a member.

12 U.S.C. § 3304. Costs and expenses of Council

One-fifth of the costs and expenses of the Council, including the salaries of its employees, shall be paid by each of the Federal financial institutions regulatory agencies. Annual assessments for such share shall be levied by the Council based upon its projected budget for the year, and additional assessments may be made during the year, if necessary.

12 U.S.C. § 3305. Functions of Council

(a) Establishment of principles and standards

The Council shall establish uniform principles and standards and report forms for the examination of financial institutions which shall be applied by the Federal financial institutions regulatory agencies.

(b) Making recommendations regarding supervisory matters and adequacy of supervisory tools

(1) The Council shall make recommendations for uniformity in other supervisory matters, such as, but not limited to, classifying loans subject to country risk, identifying financial institutions in need of special supervisory attention, and evaluating the soundness of large loans that are shared by two or more financial institutions. In addition, the Council shall make recommendations regarding the adequacy of supervisory tools for determining the impact of holding company operations on the financial institutions within the holding company and shall consider the ability of supervisory agencies to discover possible fraud or questionable and illegal payments and

practices which might occur in the operation of financial institutions or their holding companies.

(2) When a recommendation of the Council is found unacceptable by one or more of the applicable Federal financial institutions regulatory agencies, the agency or agencies shall submit to the Council, within a time period specified by the Council, a written statement of the reasons the recommendation is unacceptable.

(c) Development of uniform reporting system

The Council shall develop uniform reporting systems for federally supervised financial institutions, their holding companies, and non-financial institution subsidiaries of such institutions or holding companies. The authority to develop uniform reporting systems shall not restrict or amend the requirements of section 78l(i) of Title 15.

(d) Conducting schools for examiners and assistant examiners

The Council shall conduct schools for examiners and assistant examiners employed by the Federal financial institutions regulatory agencies. Such schools shall be open to enrollment by employees of State financial institutions supervisory agencies and employees of the Federal Housing Finance Board under conditions specified by the Council.

(e) Affect on Federal regulatory agency research and development of new financial institutions supervisory agencies

Nothing in this chapter shall be construed to limit or discourage Federal regulatory agency research and development of new financial institutions supervisory methods and tools, nor to preclude the field testing of any innovation devised by any Federal regulatory agency.

(f) Annual report

Not later than April 1 of each year, the Council shall prepare an annual report covering its activities during the preceding year.

(g) Flood insurance

The Council shall consult with and assist the Federal entities for lending regulation, as such term is defined in section 4121(a) of Title 42, in developing and coordinating uniform standards and requirements for use by regulated lending institutions under the national flood insurance program.

12 U.S.C. § 3306. State liaison

To encourage the application of uniform examination principles and standards by State and Federal supervisory agencies, the Council shall establish a liaison committee composed of five representatives of State agencies which supervise financial institutions which shall meet at least twice a year with the Council. Members of the liaison committee shall receive a reasonable allowance for necessary expenses incurred in attending meetings.

Members of the Liaison Committee shall elect a chairperson from among the members serving on the committee.

12 U.S.C. § 3307. Administration

(a) Authority of Chairman of Council

The Chairman of the Council is authorized to carry out and to delegate the authority to carry out the internal administration of the Council, including the appointment and supervision of employees and the distribution of business among members, employees, and administrative units.

(b) Use of personnel, services, and facilities of Federal financial institutions regulatory agencies, Federal Reserve banks, and Federal Home Loan Banks.

In addition to any other authority conferred upon it by this chapter, in carrying out its functions under this chapter, the Council may utilize, with their consent and to the extent practical, the personnel, services, and facilities of the Federal financial institutions regulatory agencies, Federal Reserve banks, and Federal Home Loan Banks, with or without reimbursement therefore.

(c) Compensation, authority, and duties of officers and employees; experts and consultants

In addition, the Council may—

(1) subject to the provisions of Title 5 relating to the competitive service, classification, and General Schedule pay rates, appoint and fix the compensation of such officers and employees as are necessary to carry out the provisions of this chapter, and to prescribe the authority and duties of such officers and employees; and

(2) obtain the services of such experts and consultants as are necessary to carry out the provisions of this chapter.

12 U.S.C. § 3308. Access to books, accounts, records, etc., by Council

For the purpose of carrying out this chapter, the Council shall have access to all books, accounts, records, reports, files, memorandums, papers, things, and property belonging to or in use by Federal financial institutions regulatory agencies, including reports of examination of financial institutions or their holding companies from whatever source, together with workpapers and correspondence files related to such reports, whether or not a part of the report, and all without any deletions.

12 U.S.C. § 3309. Risk management training

(a) Seminars

The Council shall develop and administer training seminars in risk management for its employees and the employees of insured financial institutions.

(b) Study of risk management training program

Not later than end of the 1-year period beginning on August 9, 1989, the Council shall—

(1) conduct a study on the feasibility and appropriateness of establishing a formalized risk management training program designed to lead to the certification of Risk Management Analysts; and

(2) report to the Congress the results of such study.

12 U.S.C. § 3310. Establishment of Appraisal Subcommittee

There shall be within the Council a subcommittee to be known as the "Appraisal Subcommittee," which shall consist of the designees of the heads of the Federal financial institutions regulatory agencies. Each such designee shall be a person who has demonstrated knowledge and competence concerning the appraisal profession.

12 U.S.C. § 3311. Required review of regulations

(a) In general

Not less frequently than once every 10 years, the Council and each appropriate Federal banking agency represented on the Council shall conduct a review of all regulations prescribed by the Council or by any such appropriate Federal banking agency, respectively, in order to identify outdated or otherwise unnecessary regulatory requirements imposed on insured depository institutions.

(b) Process

In conducting the review under subsection (a) of this section, the Council or the appropriate Federal banking agency shall—

(1) categorize the regulations described in subsection (a) of this section by type (such as consumer regulations, safety and soundness regulations, or such other des-

ignations as determined by the Council, or the appropriate Federal banking agency); and

(2) at regular intervals, provide notice and solicit public comment on a particular category or categories of regulations, requesting commentators to identify areas of the regulations that are outdated, unnecessary, or unduly burdensome.

(c) Complete review

The Council or the appropriate Federal banking agency shall ensure that the notice and comment period described in subsection (b)(2) of this section is conducted with respect to all regulations described in subsection (a) of this section not less frequently than once every 10 years.

(d) Regulatory response

The Council or the appropriate Federal banking agency shall—

(1) publish in the *Federal Register* a summary of the comments received under this section, identifying significant issues raised and providing comment on such issues; and

(2) eliminate unnecessary regulations to the extent that such action is appropriate.

(e) Report to Congress

Not later than 30 days after carrying out subsection (d)(1) of this section, the Council shall submit to Congress a report, which shall include—

(1) a summary of any significant issues raised by public comments received by the Council and the appropriate Federal banking agencies under this section and the relative merits of such issues; and

(2) an analysis of whether the appropriate Federal banking agency involved is able to address the regulatory burdens associated with such issues by regulation, or whether such burdens must be addressed by legislative action.

Excerpts from Statute Governing Appraisal Subcommittee

12 U.S.C. § 3332. Functions of Appraisal Subcommittee

(a) In general

The Appraisal Subcommittee shall—

(1) monitor the requirements established by States for the certification and licensing of individuals who are qualified to perform appraisals in connection with federally related transactions, including a code of professional responsibility;

(2) monitor the requirements established by the Federal financial institutions regulatory agencies and the Resolution Trust Corporation with respect to—

(A) appraisal standards for federally related transactions under their jurisdiction, and

(B) determinations as to which federally related transactions under their jurisdiction require the services of a State certified appraiser and which require the services of a State licensed appraiser;

(3) maintain a national registry of State certified and licensed appraisers who are eligible to perform appraisals in federally related transactions; and

(4) Omitted.

(b) Monitoring and reviewing Foundation

The Appraisal Subcommittee shall monitor and review the practices, procedures, activities, and organizational structure of the Appraisal Foundation.

12 U.S.C. § 3333. Chairperson of Appraisal Subcommittee; term of Chairperson; meetings

(a) Chairperson

The Council shall select the Chairperson of the subcommittee. The term of the Chairperson shall be two years.

Excerpts from Home Mortgage Disclosure Act

12 U.S.C. § 2801. Congressional findings and declaration of purpose

(a) Findings of Congress

The Congress finds that some depository institutions have sometimes contributed to the decline of certain geographic areas by their failure pursuant to their chartering responsibilities to provide adequate home financing to qualified applicants on reasonable terms and conditions.

(b) Purpose of chapter

The purpose of this chapter is to provide the citizens and public officials of the United States with sufficient information to enable them to determine whether depository institutions are filling their obligations to serve the housing needs of the communities and neighborhoods in which they are located and to assist public officials in their determination of the distribution of public sector investments in a manner designed to improve the private investment environment.

(c) Construction of chapter

Nothing in this chapter is intended to, nor shall it be construed to, encourage unsound lending practices or the allocation of credit.

12 U.S.C. § 2803. Maintenance of records and public disclosure

(f) Data disclosure system; operation, etc.

The Federal Financial Institutions Examination Council, in consultation with the Secretary, shall implement a system to facilitate access to data required to be disclosed under this section. Such system shall include arrangements for a central depository of data in each primary metropolitan statistical area, metropolitan statistical area, or consolidated metropolitan statistical area that is not comprised of designated primary metropolitan statistical areas. Disclosure statements shall be made available to the public for inspection and copying at such central depository of data for all depository institutions which are required to disclose information under this section (or which are exempted pursuant to section 2805(b) of this title) and which have a home office or branch office within such primary metropolitan statistical area, metropolitan statistical area, or consolidated metropolitan statistical area that is not comprised of designated primary metropolitan statistical areas.

12 U.S.C. § 2809. Compilation of aggregate data

(a) Commencement; scope of data and tables

Beginning with data for calendar year 1980, the Federal Financial Institutions Examination Council shall compile each year, for each primary metropolitan statistical area, metropolitan statistical area, or consolidated metropolitan statistical area that is not comprised of designated primary metropolitan statistical areas, aggregate data by census tract for all depository institutions which are required to disclose data under section 2803 of this title or which are exempt pursuant to section 2805(b) of this title. The Council shall also produce tables indicating, for each primary metropolitan statistical area, metropolitan statistical area, or consolidated metropolitan statistical area that is not comprised of designated primary metropolitan statistical areas, aggregate lending patterns for various categories of census tracts grouped according to location, age of housing stock, income level, and racial characteristics.

(b) Staff and data processing resources

The Board shall provide staff and data processing resources to the Council to enable it to carry out the provisions of subsection (a) of this section.

(c) Availability to public

The data and tables required pursuant to subsection (a) of this section shall be made available to the public no later than December 31 of the year following the calendar year on which the data is based.

S.A.F.E. Mortgage Licensing Act

Pub. L. No. 110-289, sections 1501, 1507 (to be codified at 12 U.S.C. § 5101, 5106, April 2009):

12 U.S.C. § 5101. Purposes and methods for establishing a mortgage licensing system and registry

In order to increase uniformity, reduce regulatory burden, enhance consumer protection, and reduce fraud, the States, through the Conference of State Bank Supervisors and the American Association of Residential Mortgage Regulators, are hereby encouraged to establish a Nationwide Mortgage Licensing System and Registry for the residential mortgage industry that accomplishes all of the following objectives:

(1) Provides uniform license applications and reporting requirements for State-licensed loan originators.

(2) Provides a comprehensive licensing and supervisory database.

(3) Aggregates and improves the flow of information to and between regulators.

(4) Provides increased accountability and tracking of loan originators.

(5) Streamlines the licensing process and reduces the regulatory burden.

(6) Enhances consumer protections and supports anti-fraud measures.

(7) Provides consumers with easily accessible information, offered at no charge, utilizing electronic media, including the Internet, regarding the employment history of, and publicly adjudicated disciplinary and enforcement actions against, loan originators.

(8) Establishes a means by which residential mortgage loan originators would, to the greatest extent possible, be required to act in the best interests of the consumer.

(9) Facilitates responsible behavior in the subprime mortgage market place and provides comprehensive training and examination requirements related to subprime mortgage lending.

(10) Facilitates the collection and disbursement of consumer complaints on behalf of State and Federal mortgage regulators.

12 U.S.C. § 5106. System of registration administration by Federal agencies

(a) Development

(1) In general

The Federal banking agencies shall jointly, through the Federal Financial Institutions Examination Council, and together with the Farm Credit Administration, develop and maintain a system for registering employees of a depository institution, employees of a subsidiary that is owned and controlled by a depository institution and regulated by a Federal banking agency, or employee of an institution regulated by the Farm Credit Administration, as registered loan originators with the Nationwide Mortgage Licensing System and Registry. The system shall be implemented before the end of the 1-year period beginning on the date of enactment of this title.

(2) Registration requirements

In connection with the registration of any loan originator under this subsection, the appropriate Federal banking agency and the Farm Credit Administration shall, at a minimum, furnish or cause to be furnished to the Nationwide Mortgage Licensing System and Registry information concerning the employees' identity, including-

(A) fingerprints for submission to the Federal Bureau of Investigation, and any governmental agency or entity authorized to receive such information for a State and national criminal history background check; and

(B) personal history and experience, including authorization for the Nationwide Mortgage Licensing System and Registry to obtain information related to any administrative, civil or criminal findings by any governmental jurisdiction.

(b) Coordination

(1) Unique identifier

The Federal banking agencies, through the Financial Institutions Examination Council, and the Farm Credit Administration shall coordinate with the Nationwide Mortgage Licensing System and Registry to establish protocols for assigning a unique identifier to each registered loan originator that will facilitate electronic tracking and uniform identification of, and public access to, the employment history of and publicly adjudicated disciplinary and enforcement actions against loan originators.

(2) Nationwide Mortgage Licensing System and Registry development

To facilitate the transfer of information required by subsection (a)(2), the Nationwide Mortgage Licensing System and Registry shall coordinate with the Federal banking agencies, through the Financial Institutions Examination Council, and the Farm Credit Administration concerning the development and operation, by such System and Registry, of the registration functionality and data requirements for loan originators.

(c) Consideration of factors and procedures

In establishing the registration procedures under subsection (a) and the protocols for assigning a unique identifier to a registered loan originator, the Federal banking agencies shall make such de minimis exceptions as may be appropriate to paragraphs (1)(A) and (2) of section 1504(a), shall make reasonable efforts to utilize existing information to minimize the burden of registering loan originators, and shall consider methods for automating the process to the greatest extent practicable consistent with the purposes of this title.

Deloitte.

INDEPENDENT AUDITORS' REPORT

The Federal Financial Institutions Examinations Council:

We have audited the accompanying balance sheets of the Federal Financial Institutions Examinations Council (the "Council") as of December 31, 2008 and 2007, and the related statements of revenues and expenses and changes in the cumulative results of operations, and cash flows for the years then ended. These financial statements are the responsibility of the Council's management. Our responsibility is to express an opinion on these financial statements based on our audits.

We conducted our audits in accordance with auditing standards generally accepted in the United States of America and the standards applicable to financial audits contained in *Government Auditing Standards* issued by the Comptroller General of the United States. Those standards require that we plan and perform the audit to obtain reasonable assurance about whether the respective financial statements are free of material misstatement. An audit includes consideration of internal control over financial reporting as a basis for designing audit procedures that are appropriate in the circumstances, but not for the purpose of expressing an opinion on the effectiveness of the Council's internal control over financial reporting. Accordingly, we express no such opinion. An audit includes examining, on a test basis, evidence supporting the amounts and disclosures in the respective financial statements, assessing the accounting principles used and significant estimates made by management, as well as evaluating the overall financial statement presentation. We believe that our audits provide a reasonable basis for our opinion.

In our opinion, such financial statements present fairly, in all material respects, the financial position of the Federal Financial Institutions Examinations Council as of December 31, 2008 and 2007, and the results of its operations and its cash flows for the years then ended in conformity with accounting principles generally accepted in the United States of America.

In accordance with *Government Auditing Standards*, we have also issued our report dated March 6, 2009, on our consideration of the Council's internal control over financial reporting and our tests of its compliance with certain provisions of laws, regulations, contracts, and grant agreements and other matters. The purpose of that report is to describe the scope of our testing of internal control over financial reporting and compliance and the results of that testing, and not to provide an opinion on the internal control over financial reporting or on compliance. That report is an integral part of an audit performed in accordance with *Government Auditing Standards* and should be considered in assessing the results of our audit.

Deloitte + Touche LLP

McLean, VA
March 6, 2009

FEDERAL FINANCIAL INSTITUTIONS EXAMINATION COUNCIL
Balance Sheets

	For the years ended December 31,	
	2008	2007

ASSETS
CURRENT ASSETS

Cash	$ 708,677	$ 838,171
Accounts receivable from member organizations (Note 3)	1,572,136	1,613,866
Other accounts receivable, net (Note 2)	105,623	256,897
Total current assets	2,386,436	2,708,934

CAPITAL ASSETS

Furniture and equipment, at cost	24,199	56,121
Central Data Repository, at cost (Note 4)	16,036,559	15,141,191
HMDA Software, at cost (Note 3)	1,544,895	745,110
Less accumulated depreciation	(7,887,093)	(5,421,241)
Net capital assets	9,718,560	10,521,181
Total assets	$ 12,104,996	$ 13,230,115

LIABILITIES AND CUMULATIVE RESULTS OF OPERATIONS

CURRENT LIABILITIES

Accounts payable and accrued liabilities payable to member organizations (Note 3)	$ 1,300,718	$ 1,148,794
Other accounts payable and accrued liabilities (Note 4)	652,538	1,251,530
Accrued payroll and annual leave	22,008	231,451
Deferred revenue (current portion) (Note 4)	3,388,881	2,497,774
Total current liabilities	5,364,145	5,129,549

LONG-TERM LIABILITIES

Deferred revenue (non-current portion) (Notes 3 and 4)	6,579,680	8,023,407
Deferred rent (Note 5)	0	32,515
Total long-term liabilities	6,579,680	8,055,922
Total liabilities	11,943,825	13,185,471

CUMULATIVE RESULTS OF OPERATIONS

	161,171	44,644
Total liabilities and cumulative results of operations	$ 12,104,996	$ 13,230,115

See accompanying notes to financial statements.

FEDERAL FINANCIAL INSTITUTIONS EXAMINATION COUNCIL
Statements of Revenues and Expenses and Changes in Cumulative Results of Operations

	For the years ended December 31,	
	2008	2007
REVENUES		
Assessments on member organizations (Note 3)	$ 574,447	$ 540,813
Central Data Repository (Note 4)	6,160,478	5,723,376
Home Mortgage Disclosure (Note 6)	2,969,535	2,830,584
Tuition (Note 3)	1,744,029	2,141,331
Community Reinvestment Act (Note 6)	931,244	881,953
Uniform Bank Performance Report (Note 6)	565,522	585,973
Appraisal Subcommittee (Note 6)	178,963	216,556
Total revenues	13,124,218	12,920,586
EXPENSES		
Data processing	4,126,928	3,988,462
Professional fees (Note 4)	4,261,260	4,057,023
Salaries and related benefits (Note 3)	1,164,304	1,374,193
Depreciation (Note 4)	2,497,774	2,474,070
Rental of office space (Note7)	454,184	516,364
Administration fees (Note 3)	190,400	190,800
Travel	135,006	120,181
Books and subscriptions	16,255	96,696
Other seminar expenses	30,824	21,571
Rental and maintenance of office equipment	41,998	56,598
Office and other supplies	33,980	26,686
Printing	43,261	27,099
Postage	2,475	5,075
Miscellaneous	9,042	4,514
Total expenses	13,007,691	12,959,332
RESULTS OF OPERATIONS	116,527	(38,746)
CUMULATIVE RESULTS OF OPERATIONS, Beginning of period	44,644	83,390
CUMULATIVE RESULTS OF OPERATIONS, End of period	$ 161,171	$ 44,644

See accompanying notes to financial statements.

FEDERAL FINANCIAL INSTITUTIONS EXAMINATION COUNCIL
Statements of Cash Flows

	For the years ended December 31,	
	2008	2007
CASH FLOWS FROM OPERATING ACTIVITIES		
RESULTS OF OPERATIONS	$ 116,527	$ (38,746)
Adjustments to reconcile results of operations to net cash provided by operating activities:		
Depreciation	2,497,774	2,474,070
Central Data Repository write-off	1,068,697	0
(Increase) decrease in assets:		
Accounts receivable from member organizations	41,730	(616,524)
Other accounts receivable	151,274	(13,717)
Increase (decrease) in liabilities:		
Accounts payable and accrued liabilities payable to member organizations	151,924	351,701
Other accounts payable and accrued liabilities	(598,992)	606,092
Accrued payroll and annual leave	(209,443)	(81,587)
Deferred revenue (current and non-current)	(552,620)	506,896
Deferred rent	(32,515)	(25,648)
Net cash provided by operating activities	2,634,356	3,162,537
CASH FLOWS FROM INVESTING ACTIVITIES		
Capital expenditures	(2,763,850)	(2,980,966)
Net cash used in investing activities	(2,763,850)	(2,980,966)
NET (DECREASE) INCREASE IN CASH	(129,494)	181,571
CASH BALANCE, Beginning of period	838,171	656,600
CASH BALANCE, End of period	$ 708,677	$ 838,171

See accompanying notes to financial statements.

Notes to Financial Statements as of and for the Years Ended December 31, 2008 and 2007

1. Organization and Purpose

The Federal Financial Institutions Examination Council (the "Council") was established under Title X of the Financial Institutions Regulatory and Interest Rate Control Act of 1978. The purpose of the Council is to prescribe uniform principles and standards for the federal examination of financial institutions and to make recommendations to promote uniformity in the supervision of these financial institutions. The five agencies which are represented on the Council, referred to hereinafter as member organizations, are as follows:

Board of Governors of the Federal Reserve System (FRB)
Federal Deposit Insurance Corporation (FDIC)
National Credit Union Administration (NCUA)
Office of the Comptroller of the Currency (OCC)
Office of Thrift Supervision (OTS)

In accordance with the Financial Services Regulatory Relief Act of 2006, a representative state regulator was added as a full voting member of the FFIEC in October 2006.

The Council was given additional statutory responsibilities by section 340 of the Housing and Community Development Act of 1980, Public Law 96-399. Among these responsibilities are the implementation of a system to facilitate public access to data that depository institutions must disclose under the Home Mortgage Disclosure Act of 1975 (HMDA) and the aggregation of annual HMDA data, by census tract, for each metropolitan statistical area.

Appraisal Subcommittee—The Council's financial statements do not include financial data for the Appraisal Subcommittee. The Appraisal Subcommittee of the Council was created pursuant to Public Law 101-73, Title XI of the Financial Institutions Reform, Recovery, and Enforcement Act of 1989. The functions of the Appraisal Subcommittee are related to the certification and licensing of individuals who perform appraisals in connection with federally related real estate transactions. Members of the Appraisal Subcommittee consist of the designees of the heads of those agencies which comprise the Council and the designee of the head of the Department of Housing and Urban Development.

All functions and responsibilities assigned to the Council under Title XI are performed directly by the Appraisal Subcommittee without any need for approval or concurrence from the Council. The Appraisal Subcommittee has its own policies and procedures and submits its own Annual Report to the President of the Senate and Speaker of the House. The Council is not responsible for any debts incurred by the Subcommittee, nor are Subcommittee funds available for use by the Council.

2. Significant Accounting Policies

The Council prepares its financial statements in accordance with accounting principles generally accepted in the United States based upon accounting standards issued by the Financial Accounting Standards Board (FASB).

Revenues—Assessments made on member organizations for operating expenses and additions to property are based on expected cash needs. Amounts over- or under- assessed due to differences between actual and expected cash needs flow into "Cumulative Results of Operations" during the year and then are used to offset or increase the next year's assessment. Deficits in "Cumulative Results of Operations" can be made up in the following year's assessments.

Tuition revenue is adjusted at year-end to match expenses incurred as a result of providing education classes. For differences between revenues and expenses, member agencies are billed an additional amount or credited a refund based on each member's proportional cost for the Examiner Education budget.

Capital Assets—Furniture and equipment is recorded at cost less accumulated depreciation. Depreciation is calculated on a straight-line basis over the estimated useful lives of the assets, which range from four to ten years. Upon the sale or other disposition of a depreciable asset, the cost and related accumulated depreciation are removed from the accounts and any gain or loss is recognized. The Central Data Repository (CDR), an internally developed software project, is recorded at cost in accordance with Statement of Position 98-1, *Accounting for the Costs of Computer Software Developed or Obtained for Internal Use.* (See Note 4)

Deferred Revenue—Deferred revenue includes cash collected and accounts receivable primarily related to the CDR and Home Mortgage Disclosure Act (HMDA). (See Notes 3 and 4)

Estimates—The preparation of financial statements in conformity with accounting principles generally accepted in the United States requires management to make estimates and assumptions that affect the reported amounts of assets and liabilities and the disclosure of contingent assets and liabilities at the date of the financial statements and the reported amounts of revenues and expenses during the reporting period. Actual results could differ from those estimates.

Allowance for Doubtful Accounts—Accounts receivable are shown net of the allowance for doubtful accounts. Accounts receivable considered uncollectible are charged against the allowance account in the year they are deemed uncollectible. The allowance for doubtful accounts is adjusted monthly, based upon a review of outstanding receivables.

3. Transactions with Member Organizations

	2008	2007
Accounts Receivable		
Board of Governors of the Federal Reserve System	$ 373,466	$ 343,739
Federal Deposit Insurance Corporation	466,052	434,908
National Credit Union Administration	109,261	97,765

	2008	2007
Office of the Comptroller of the Currency	$ 522,167	$ 500,397
Office of Thrift Supervision	101,190	237,057
	$ 1,572,136	$ 1,613,866
Accounts Payable and Accrued Liabilities		
Board of Governors of the Federal Reserve System	$ 650,672	$ 532,047
Federal Deposit Insurance Corporation	396,899	182,491
National Credit Union Administration	40,085	66,342
Office of the Comptroller of the Currency	132,891	344,659
Office of Thrift Supervision	80,171	23,255
	$ 1,300,718	$ 1,148,794
Operations		
Assessments to member organizations for operating expenses	$ 574,447	$ 540,813
FRB provided administrative support services to the Council at an expense of:	$ 190,400	$ 190,800

The Council does not directly employ personnel, but rather member organizations detail personnel to support Council operations. These personnel are paid through the payroll systems of member organizations. Salaries and fringe benefits, including retirement benefit plan contributions, are reimbursed to these organizations. The Council does not have any post-retirement or post-employment benefit liabilities since Council personnel are included in the plans of the member organizations.

Member organizations are not reimbursed for the costs of personnel who serve as Council members and on the various task forces and committees of the Council. The value of these contributed services is not included in the accompanying financial statements.

Examiner Education

The Council provides seminars in the Washington, D.C. area and at regional locations throughout the country for member organization examiners and other agencies. Tuition revenue earned from member organizations was:	$ 1,627,429	$ 2,036,000

Notes continue on the following page.

	2008	2007

Other Member Expenses

Member organizations provide office space and data processing services to the Council at an expense of: $ 4,374,577 $ 3,945,705

HMDA Deferred Revenue

In 2007, the Council began a rewrite of the entire HMDA processing system. The total estimated cost for the rewrite is $3.2 million over 3.5 years. The cost of the software in process is $1,544,895 and $745,110 as of December 31, 2008 and 2007, respectively.

UBPR

The Council coordinates the production and distribution of the Uniform Bank Performance Reports (UBPR) through the FDIC. The Council is reimbursed for the direct cost of the operating expenses it incurs for this project.

4. Central Data Repository

In 2003, the Council entered into an agreement with UNISYS, totaling approximately $40 million, to enhance the methods and systems used to collect, validate, process, and distribute Call Report information, and to store this information in a Central Data Repository (CDR).

The CDR was placed into service in October 2005. At that time, the Council began depreciating the CDR project on the straight-line basis over its estimated useful life of sixty-three months. The Council records depreciation expenses and recognizes the same amount of deferred revenue. The value of the CDR asset includes the fully accrued and paid cost.

	2008	2007
Capital Asset CDR		
Beginning balance	$12,858,440	$12,313,244
Software placed in use during the year	1,282,215	545,196
Software in use	14,140,655	12,858,440
Software in development	1,895,904	2,282,751
Total asset	$16,036,559	$15,141,191

Other Accounts Payable and Accrued Liabilities

Payable to UNISYS for the CDR project	$ 609,203	$ 841,392
Other vendors unrelated to the CDR project	43,335	410,138
Total other accounts payable and accrued liabilities	$ 652,538	$ 1,251,530

Revenues-Central Data Repository—The Council is funding the project by billing the three par-

ticipating Council member organizations (FRB, FDIC, and OCC).

	2008	2007
Deferred Revenue		
Beginning balance	$ 9,776,071	$10,014,285
Additions	895,369	2,235,856
Less: Revenue recognized	(2,497,774)	(2,474,070)
Ending balance	$ 8,173,666	$ 9,776,071
Current portion deferred revenue	$ 3,138,881	$ 2,497,774
Long-term deferred revenue	5,034,785	7,278,297
	$ 8,173,666	$ 9,776,071
Total CDR Revenue		
Deferred revenue	$ 2,497,774	$ 2,474,070
Hosting and maintenance fees	3,662,704	3,249,306
Total CDR revenue	$ 6,160,478	$ 5,723,376
Professional Fees		
Hosting and maintenance fees for the CDR project	$ 3,662,704	$ 3,249,306
Other professional fees unrelated to the CDR project	598,556	807,717
Total professional fees	$ 4,261,260	$ 4,057,023
Depreciation		
Depreciation for the CDR project	$ 2,497,774	$ 2,474,070
Average monthly amortization	$ 208,148	$ 206,173

5. Deferred Rent

In 2005, the Council entered into a lease for office and classroom space that contains scheduled rent increases over the term of the lease. In accordance with accounting principles generally accepted in the United States, rent abatements and scheduled rent increases must be considered in determining the annual rent expense to be recognized. The deferred rent represents the difference between the actual lease payments and the rent expense recognized.

6. Other Revenue

	2008	2007
Home Mortgage Disclosure Act (HMDA)		
The Council recognized the following revenue from member organizations for the production and distribution of reports under the HMDA:	$ 2,088,052	$ 1,857,454

	2008	2007
The Council recognized the following revenue from the Department of Housing and Urban Development's participation in the HMDA project:	600,089	699,663
The Council recognized the following revenue from the Mortgage Insurance Companies of America for performing HMDA-related work:	264,193	258,986
The balance of the HMDA revenue for 2008 and 2007 was from sales to the public:	17,201	14,481
Total HMDA	$ 2,969,535	$ 2,830,584

Community Reinvestment Act (CRA)—The Council recognized revenue for support of operating expenses from the participating member agencies.

Uniform Bank Performance Report (UBPR)—The Council recognized revenue for coordinating and providing certain administrative support to the UBPR project.

Appraisal Subcommittee—The Council recognized revenue for providing space to the Appraisal Subcommittee.

7. Operating Leases

The FRB, on behalf of the Council, entered into two operating leases to secure office and classroom space. One lease terminated in 2008 and the other terminates in 2009 with a lease extension option of five years. Rental expenses under these operating leases were $454,184 and $516,364 as of December 31, 2008 and 2007, respectively. The minimum lease payments for 2009 are estimated to be $255,261.

Deloitte.

INDEPENDENT AUDITORS' REPORT ON COMPLIANCE AND ON INTERNAL CONTROL OVER FINANCIAL REPORTING BASED ON AN AUDIT OF FINANCIAL STATEMENTS PERFORMED IN ACCORDANCE WITH GOVERNMENT AUDITING STANDARDS

To The Federal Financial Institutions Examination Council:

We have audited the financial statements of the Financial Institutions Examination Council (the "Council") as of and for the year ended December 31, 2008, and have issued our report thereon dated March 6, 2009. We conducted our audit in accordance with auditing standards generally accepted in the United States of America and the standards applicable to financial audits contained in *Government Auditing Standards*, issued by the Comptroller General of the United States.

Internal Control over Financial Reporting

In planning and performing our audit, we considered the Council's internal control over financial reporting in order to determine our auditing procedures for the purpose of expressing our opinion on the financial statements and not to provide assurance on the internal control over financial reporting. Our consideration of the internal control over financial reporting would not necessarily disclose all matters in the internal control that might be material weaknesses. A material weakness is a condition in which the design or operation of one or more of the internal control components does not reduce to a relatively low level the risk that misstatements in amounts that would be material in relation to the financial statements being audited may occur and not be detected within a timely period by employees in the normal course of performing their assigned functions. We noted no matters involving the internal control over financial reporting and its operation that we consider to be material weaknesses.

Compliance

As part of obtaining reasonable assurance about whether the Council's financial statements are free of material misstatement, we performed tests of its compliance with certain provisions of laws, regulations, contracts, and grants, noncompliance with which could have a direct and material effect on the determination of financial statement amounts. However, providing an opinion on compliance with those provisions was not an objective of our audit, and accordingly, we do not express such an opinion. The results of our tests disclosed no instances of noncompliance or other matters that are required to be reported under *Government Auditing Standards*.

Member of
Deloitte Touche Tohmatsu

35

Distribution

This report is intended solely for the information and use of the Council, management, and others within the organization, and the Office of Inspector General, and the United States Congress, and is not intended to be and should not be used by anyone other than these specified parties.

Deloitte + Touche LLP

McLean, VA
March 6, 2009

APPENDIX C: MAPS OF AGENCY REGIONS AND DISTRICTS

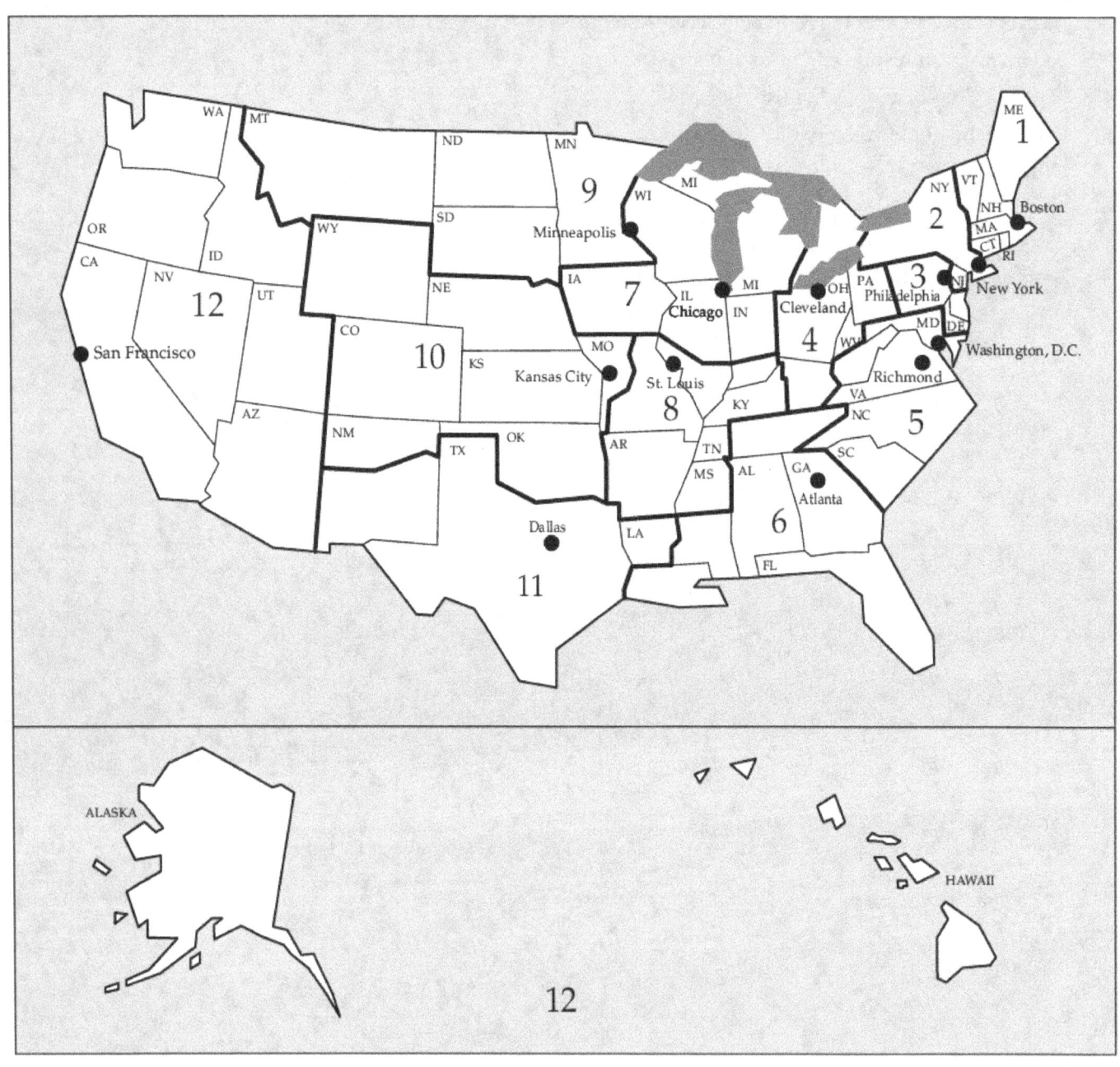

FEDERAL DEPOSIT INSURANCE CORPORATION REGIONS (SUPERVISION AND COMPLIANCE)

*   Two area offices are located in Boston
    (reports to New York) and Memphis
    (reports to Dallas)

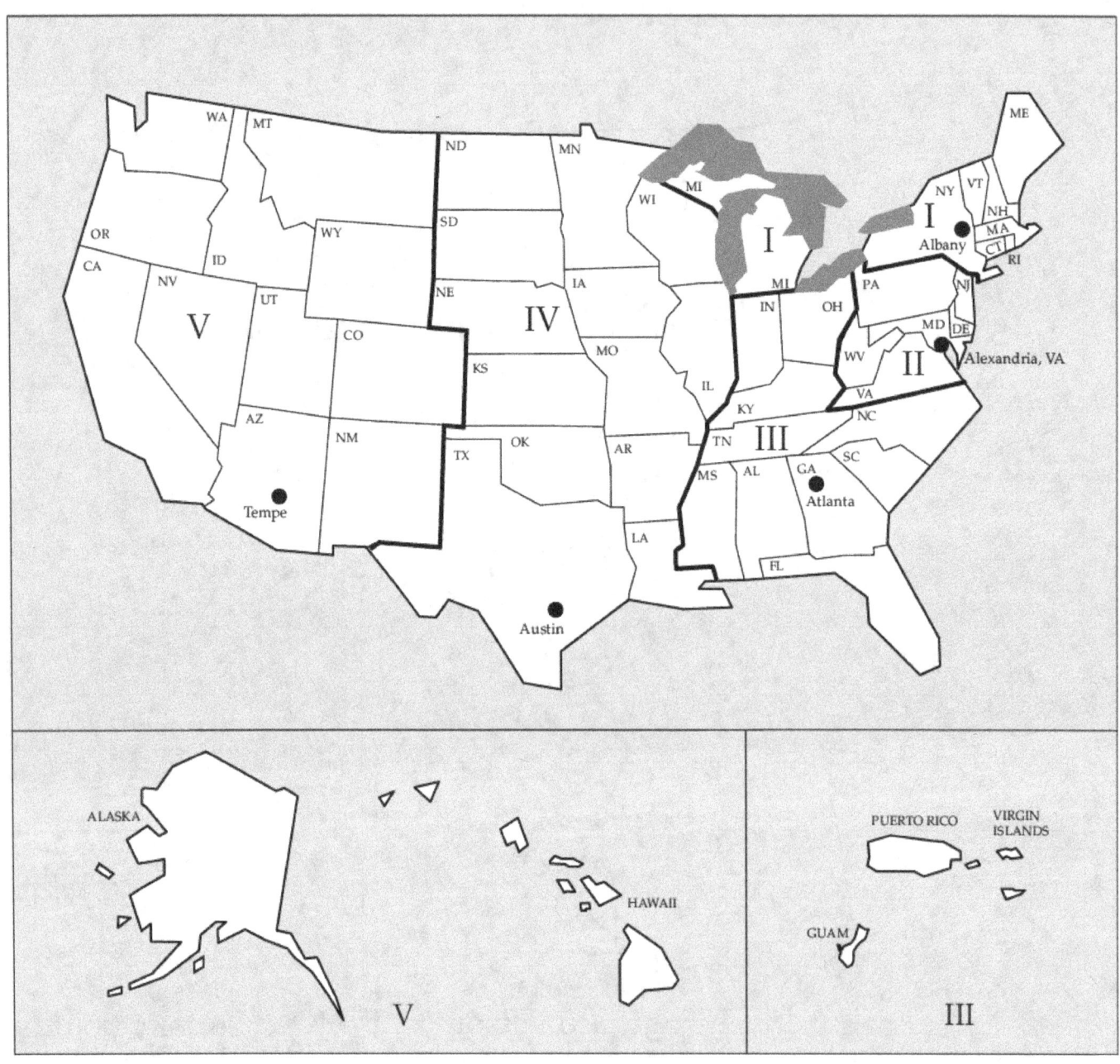

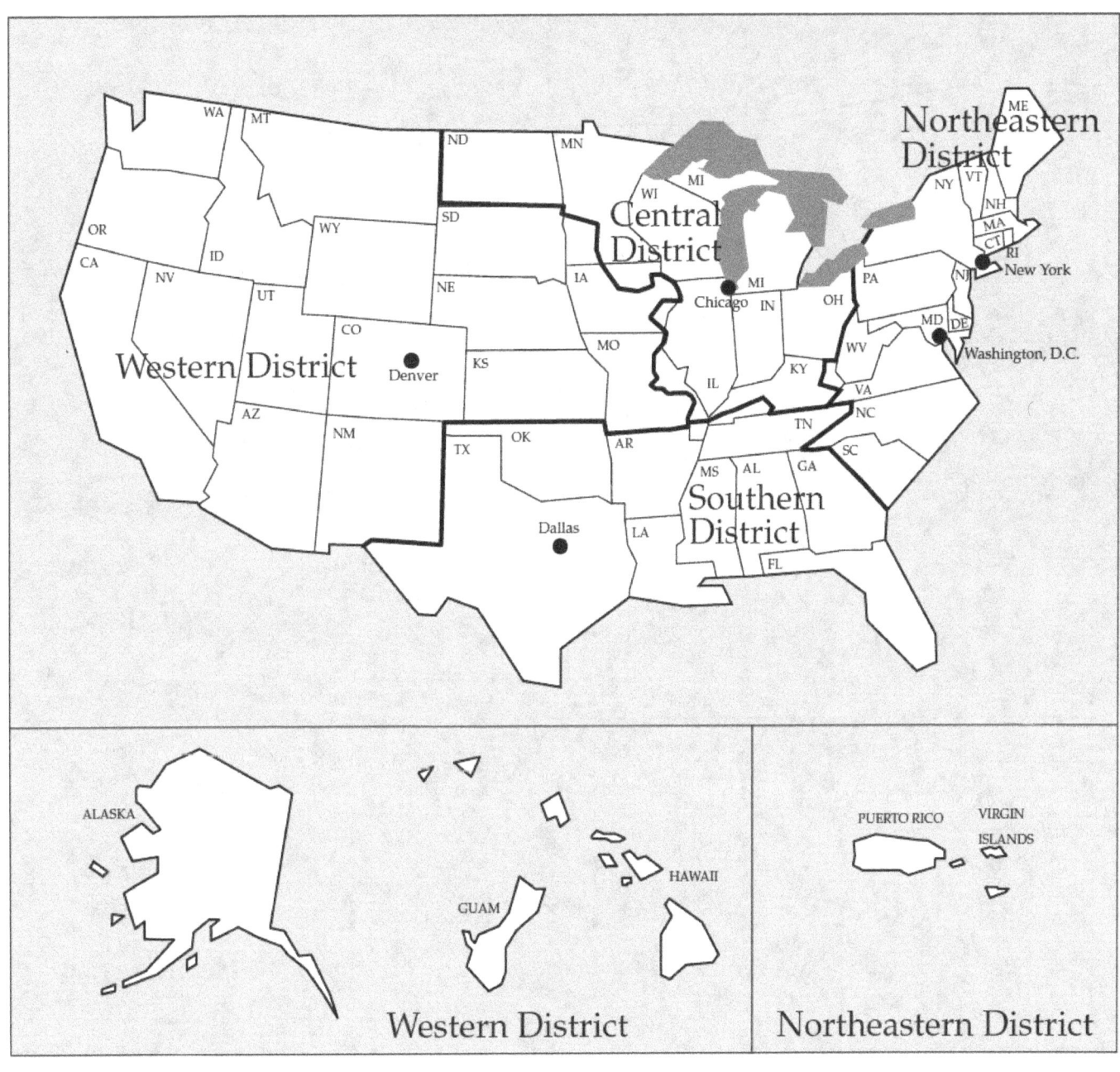

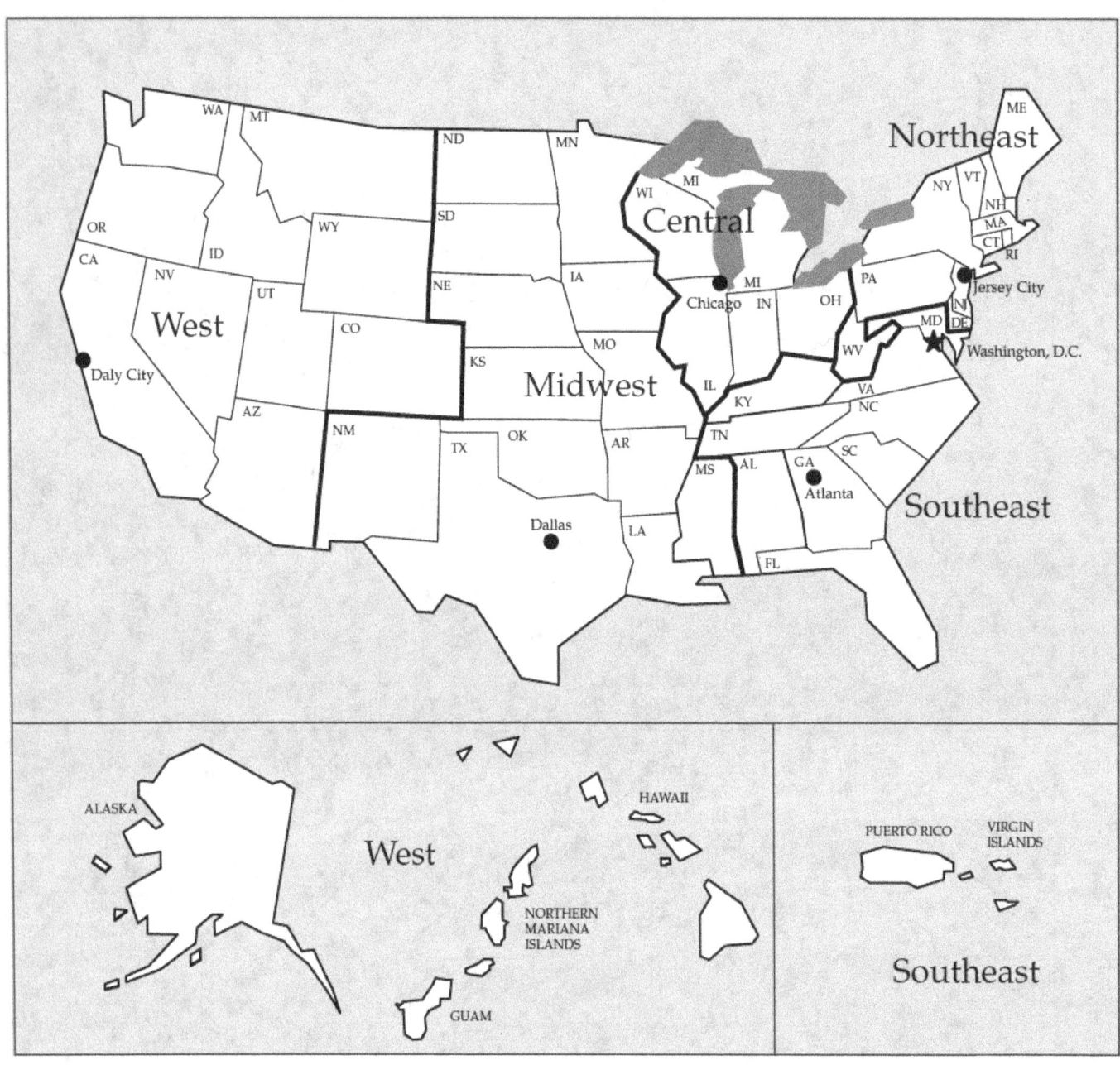

APPENDIX D: ORGANIZATIONAL LISTING OF PERSONNEL

Organization, December 31, 2008

Members of the Council

Randall Kroszner, *Chairman*
Member
Board of Governors of the Federal
Reserve System (FRB)

Sheila C. Bair, *Vice Chairman*
Chairperson
Federal Deposit Insurance
Corporation (FDIC)

John C. Dugan
Comptroller of the Currency
Office of the Comptroller of the
Currency (OCC)

Michael E. Fryzel
Chairman
National Credit Union
Administration (NCUA)

John Munn
State Liaison Committee
Chairman
Director
Nebraska Department of Banking
& Finance

John M. Reich
Director
Office of Thrift Supervision (OTS)

State Liaison Committee (SLC)

John Munn, *Chairman*
Director
Nebraska Department of Banking
& Finance

Sandra Branson
Director
Missouri Division of Credit
Unions

D. Eric McClure
Commissioner
Missouri Division of Finance

Mick Thompson
Commissioner
Oklahoma State Banking
Department

Doug Foster
Commissioner
Texas Department of Savings &
Mortgage Lending

Council Staff Officer

Paul T. Sanford
Executive Secretary

Interagency Staff Groups

Agency Liaison Group

Roger T. Cole (FRB)
Tim Long (OCC)
David M. Marquis (NCUA)
Michael Stevens (SLC Chair
Representative)
Sandra Thompson (FDIC)
Timothy T. Ward (OTS)

Legal Advisory Group

Scott Alvarez, *Chairman* (FRB)
John Bowman (OTS)
Robert M. Fenner (NCUA)
Gavin Gee (SLC Chair
Representative)
Sara A. Kelsey (FDIC), retired 10/08
Julie L. Williams (OCC)

Task Force on Consumer Compliance

Luke H. Brown, *Chairman* (FDIC)
Matthew Bilouris (NCUA)
David Cotney (SLC Chair
Representative)
Ann Jaedicke (OCC)
Glenn Loney (FRB)
Montrice G. Yakimov (OTS)

Task Force on Examiner Education

Matthew Amato, *Chairman* (OTS)
Charlotte Buchanan (SLC Chair
Representative)
Cheryl Davis (OCC)
Joy Lee (NCUA)
Dana E. Payne (FRB)
Betty J. Rudolph (FDIC)

Task Force on Information Sharing

Robin Stefan, *Chairman* (OCC)
David Godwin (OTS)
John Kolhoff (SLC Chair
Representative)
Michael Kraemer (FRB)
Dominick Nigro (NCUA)
Jaime J. Perez (FDIC)

Task Force on Reports

Robert F. Storch, *Chairman* (FDIC)
Zane D. Blackburn (OCC)
James Caton (OTS)
Arthur Lindo (FRB)
George Reynolds (SLC Chair
Representative)
R. Ashley Rowe (NCUA)

Task Force on Supervision

Roger T. Cole, *Chairman* (FRB)
Joy Lee (NCUA)
Tim Long (OCC)
Howard Pitkin (SLC Chair
Representative)
Sandra Thompson (FDIC)
Timothy Ward (OTS)

Task Force on Surveillance Systems

Robin Stefan, *Chairman* (OCC)
Bob Bacon (SLC Chair
Representative)
James Caton (OTS)
Charles Collier (FDIC)
Matt Mattson (FRB)
R. Ashlely Rowe (NCUA)

Staff Members of the FFIEC

Shown are the FFIEC staff members at the Seidman Center in Arlington, Virginia, where they have their offices and classrooms for examiner education programs.

Federal Financial Institutions Examination Council staff members (from the left to right): Cynthia Curry-Daniel, Ernest Larkins, Michelle Clark, Rosanna Piccirilli, Paul Sanford, Darlene Callis, John Smullen, Karen Smith, Susan Saari, Juliet Pradier, Jennifer Herring, and Catherine Pritchard.